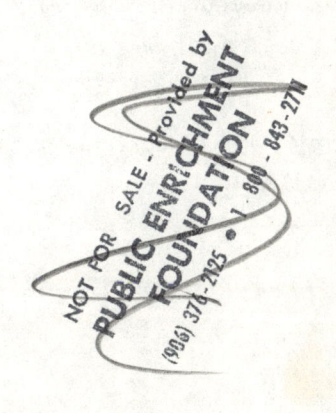

Copyright, Bob Niss, 1983

All rights reserved. No part of this work may be reproduced or transmitted in any form by any means, electronic or mechanical, including photocopying and recording, or by any information storage or retrieval system, without permission in writing from the publisher, except by a reviewer who may quote brief passages for a review.

First edition June, 1983. Printed in the United States of America by Gannett Graphics, Augusta, Maine 04330.

Published by Guy Gannett Publishing Co., Portland, Maine, 04101, June, 1983.

Library of Congress Catalog Card #83-80466
ISBN #0-930-09647-9

NEW ENGLAND NATURALLY

A Back Forty Journal
by *BOB NISS*

Guy Gannett Publishing Co.
Portland/Maine

ACKNOWLEDGEMENTS

There hardly is sufficient space — or words — to express my gratitude to each person who has had a role in the emergence of this book, but there are some whose roles cannot go unacknowledged.

Thank-you to . . .

My parents, Abby and Bill Niss, who taught me to respect and listen to the world around me.

The late Clarence E. Allen, my childhood tutor who is with me still whenever I venture into the woods.

My sons, Matt and Josh, and the other children in my life whose eyes have given me new perspectives.

Those whose encouragement, however casual, has given me the impetus to finish this project, among them Martin Dibner, Sally Arteseros, the late Edwin Way Teale, Olin Sewall Pettingill, Allan Swenson, Bunny Crowley, Joe and Mary Youngs and Dot Hill.

And finally, some of those with whom I have shared the outdoors, friends who have lent me their love and their insights: David and Sunshine Burden, Bill Phinney, Aunt Anne Frantz and Aunt Mary Bowden, Debi and Steve Neumeister, Chip Bell, Bob Naylor, Glenn Hill, Jennifer Moughalian, Jeff Peavey, Chet Main, Ray Peabody, Sarah Andrews . . .

— Bob Niss

To JUDY.

*I spent hours and days and weeks
Writing and erasing rhymes and riddles
    for this space,
But none worked; none fit;
    none said it.
They came out trite and tired.
They didn't say what they should've said.
They didn't say.... I love you.*

INTRODUCTION

This is the place where the author of a book or someone who likes him a lot is supposed to convince you that your investment was a wise one. I'm not going to do that and I'm not going to ask anyone to tell you what a saint I am. Instead, I'll simply ask you to let the book speak for itself. That way, we'll all save some energy and perhaps a few trees.

I would note for the record, however, that this book is a compendium of expanded, edited and hopefully improved columns entitled "The Back Forty" which appear regularly in *The Maine Sunday Telegram*. A good deal of new material has been integrated into the text, which can best be described as a reflection of my activities, observances and thoughts while living on and exploring a 40-acre Maine woodlot and visiting other relatively unspoiled sections of New England.

I hope you enjoy it.

— Bob Niss

NEW ENGLAND NATURALLY

A Back Forty Journal

SPRING

Symphony	3
North	9
Mud & Stuff	19
Visions	31
On Toward Summer	37

SUMMER

New Chords	59
Gathering Of Beasts	69
Skulking, Haying & Such	91
Moving On	105

AUTUMN

Bright & Dull	125
Beasts Of The Frost	147

WINTER

Snow & Ice	161
Snow Birds	173
Snow Beasts	185
Hot & Cold	193
Change	203

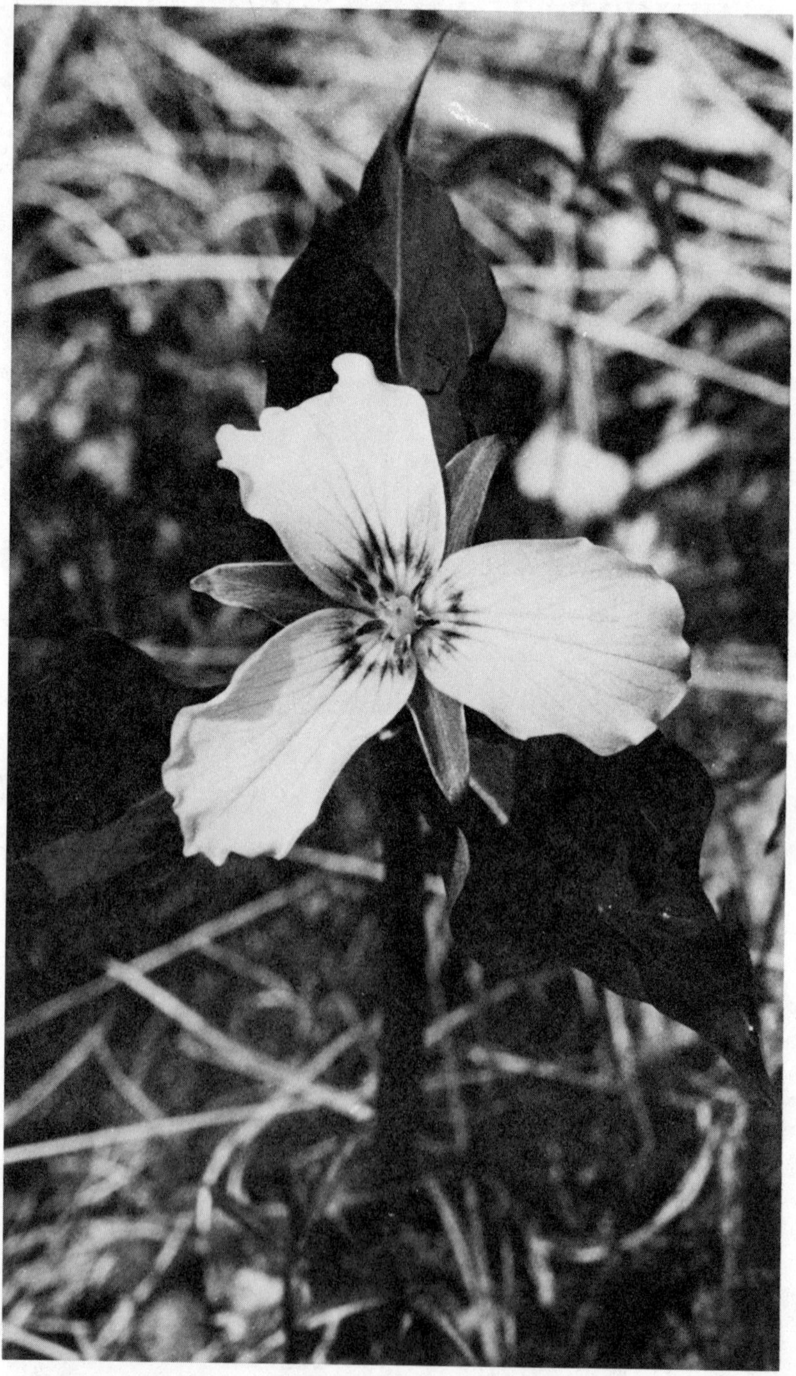

SPRING

2

Steve Bowler

SYMPHONY

It comes suddenly on the back forty, sliding softly across the ridge like the morning sun, borne on blackbirds' wings and whispering gently through the bare beech trees.

Spring is no longer a veiled promise, but a symphony of careful chords. Early March's lone flute has yielded to the strings and woodwinds of genuine spring, heralded also by the occasional clamor of brass and percussion.

The ground is still covered with snow, but it is the dirt-streaked snow of a dying winter, pock-marked with the aged, melt-distorted tracks of deer, raccoon and rabbit. It recedes quickly from the trunks of trees, as a hand pulls away from a hot ember. The earth is damp and sheathed with the moldy lace of winter's rot. Rotting, too, is the ice that has gripped the ponds since early December, unveiling the crystal-clear water that is unique to spring. The ice rots not in the manner of flesh or fiber, but rather in audible unison, disintegrating into vertical shards with the sound of countless tiny bells. Deep within the amber liquid, the first water beetles and tadpoles begin to stir with lethargic purpose.

A pair of black ducks wheels swiftly overhead, the vanguard of untold numbers that soon will be heading inland from the coastal inlets and estuaries to seek out ponds, bogs and swamps in which to raise their young. They squawk with impatience and anxiety, but they or their kin will be back to skulk among the bayberry and to fatten themselves on the plenty of spring and summer.

The first blackbird's song tumbles liquidly from the top of a pine tree and the distinctive spring song of the chickadee fills the dappled edges of the woodlot. Here and there, a fly struggles across an oasis of pine needles or rises in a sluggish, buzzing spiral into the promise-filled air. Soon, the first of the phoebes will arrive to take advantage of the early hatch and to lay claim to a barn rafter or windowsill as foundation for its mud-and-moss nest.

The sap is running, discoloring the trunks of maples and oaks beneath fresh bark wounds, attracting squirrels and chipmunks grown weary of muddied, melted snow. Everything is wet. The earth, especially at the edges of shade-prolonged snow, turns to mud beneath the feet. Small rivulets of snowmelt wander from the birch knoll to the ponds on either side, twisting and turning around boulders, stumps and dimples of earth thrust upward by meandering moles.

Spring.

The sun has crossed the equator and the earth's northern hemisphere tilts to face the burning orb. The vernal equinox.

Resurrection.

For some, the season means death. The hunting season of five months ago pushes the deer deep into the back forty and its adjoining matrix of bogs and thickets, denying them a final month of far-flung gluttony before the snows of winter. By Christmas, their territorial winter "yard" is firmly established. Only fluctuating depths of snow will assure adequate browse for the duration of the season. Following trails established by their distant forebears, they wander the yard throughout January and into February, but with the advent of March and its softening breezes, they roam farther and farther from their cloven trails. The buds and hardwood bark that sustain them within the yard have been exhausted. Spring is here, but for some it is too late. They have already crossed the thin but finite line between life and death, wandering amid the emerging plenty. A belly-filling meal only accelerates the inevitable, demanding of the body chores which it no longer can perform.

The raccoons, too, are abroad. They came throughout the winter to the birdfeeders for hasty, quarrelsome meals, but now they push into the wet pine grove beyond and onto the matted grasses flanking the ponds, probing everywhere for the living food they have done without for so many nights and days.

They and the others who share the woods can easily be fooled, however, by the gentle tenor of the rising symphony. The air of this transitory time can be filled with either snowflakes or mosquitoes. But it does not seem to matter much: the promise is clear and firm.

It is the time of spring.

It is the pond's version of the crocus and the robin song, a shrill but strangely soothing "Greek!" that pierces the foggy dusk.

Pads of ice shards, clinging to one another in a final defense against the spreading warmth, still choke the heart of the ponds, but the ice-free shallows have warmed sufficiently to awaken and attract the first spring peeper. Its awakening is more reassuring than the arrival of the first robin, perhaps because it has stayed through the winter months, sharing its perils. Its verbalizations are therefore firm statements of hope and promise . . . and fact.

Always, there is one very magical spring evening on the back forty when each and every peeper raises its voice in exuberant

Guy Gannett Publishing Co.

celebration, shaking the air with a din that is uncannily harmonious. I have heard many a symphony orchestra in my time, yet none has equalled the purity of tone and sheer melodic joy of the peepers. On that magical evening, I often lie awake into the early morning hours to listen to the symphony and on occasion I will venture to the edge of the larger pond and settle into my favorite "perch" beneath a multi-legged maple to be bathed more completely by the cascading song.

The concert continues from mid-April through May, decreasing in intensity and harmony until there is but the faintest whisper of an encore.

The frogs — tree frogs, to be precise — responsible for all this concertizing are curious creatures, tiny amphibians easily distinguished from their larger kin not only by size, but by the presence of generally sticky discs or pads at the tips of their toes and fingers. Even sheer glass is no barrier to these prodigious climbers: one especially predictable green tree frog spent at least one hour each evening for an entire week last April on a particular pane of glass in a particular window of the kitchen. I never saw it arrive or leave. It simply was there, as though congealed from the damp air.

The peepers are at once little-known and commonplace. Measuring from a miniscule half-inch long in the case of the appropriately-named little grass frog to a comparatively gargantuan four inches in the case of several species, they are obviously hard to spot. Their secrecy is exasperatingly enhanced by an ability among most to alter their skin coloration to match or mimic that of their surroundings. As if that isn't enough to assure their anonymity, they also are blessed with a keen sense of hearing that provides ample warning of approaching danger.

To find a peeper, one must usually hunt for it as though it were a lost contact lens. The only necessary equipment are a flashlight and a good reserve of patience. Stand quietly and without moving in the damp woods on a spring evening and listen. Select what appears to be the nearest "song" and step cautiously toward it. Should the songster fall silent — which is quite likely — merely wait until it or a neighbor rejoins the chorus and repeat the procedure until you're certain of the quarry's location. Aim and turn on your flashlight. You probably won't see the frog immediately, thanks to its effective camouflage and its talents as a ventriloquist, but a methodical scanning of the immediate area should ultimately disclose its location. If possible, seek out one which seems to be at work in a tree or bush: those favoring the ground can quickly vanish into any one of countless leafy, woody

Spring Peeper   Leonard Lee Rue III

sanctuaries.

    The harmonious din which the peepers raise is especially astonishing when one considers the fact that only the males vocalize, enticing females with loud displays of ardent virility. There obviously are a great many of the beasts abroad at the dawn of spring, and with good reason. Frogs of any variety are among the most hunted and otherwise threatened of all the world's animals. They must reproduce at a phenomenal rate in order to guarantee that an adequate percentage will survive to achieve sexual maturity. Adult peepers are relished by a veritable horde of predators, including herons, turtles, raccoons, foxes and other frogs. Their tadpole youngsters face comparable perils beneath the surface of the pond and even their eggs are actively hunted by the likes of specialized leeches that can wriggle into the gelatinous mass to dine on the helpless embryos.

    Thankfully, enough do escape the gauntlet to lend music and magic to the spring evening.

Guy Gannett Publishing Co.

NORTH

The nightsounds are at first perplexing. It has been a long time since I last was alone in the northwoods. There had always been people and voices in my campsites, buffers between myself and the animal din of night.

I knew I was to be alone here, hugging the fringes of the tall timber country, when I found cobwebs lacing the outhouse hole, and I was glad... not for the cobwebs, but for the solitude after a winter of outer and inner storms. But the nightsounds: I can't quite place them all, though each is familiar, like the face of a high school classmate you haven't seen for twenty years.

A snorting from the thicket of alder and scrub birch across the narrow gravel road. Moose. The forest ranger had said a bull and cow were frequenting the campground, attracted to the hundred-pound bags of calcium chloride stacked in a nearby gravel pit for use during the tourist months to combat road dust. The cow had spent the afternoon in the meadow between the campground and the river, a fair-sized animal engulfed in clouds of flies, her ragged flanks dotted with the red bulbs of ticks.

Whippoorwills. One is very close, repeating its telltale call 137... 138... 139... 140... 141 times without pause.

Snapping twigs. Animals moving through the thick brush behind the campsite.

Frogs. Deep, throaty croakings from the backwaters and marshes.

Bats. Animal twitterings blending with the constant drone of countless night insects.

Sleep comes slowly, and only with the welcome reassurance that the nightsounds are not unfamiliar after all. The night air is chill, as it most always is in these northern valleys, and the stars glitter through the tiers of dark spruce and tamarack.

Breakfast.
The crisp, star-flecked night has yielded to a dull, gray morning, filled with drizzle and erratic breezes.

Across the narrow road, the fibrous skeleton of an aged poplar serves as a way-station for many of the birds in the vicinity. At one point, somewhere between coffee and more coffee, its branches are simultaneously occupied by three cedar waxwings, two evening grosbeaks, a yellow-shafted flicker, two scarlet tanagers, a blackburnian warbler and four goldfinches. Were it a pear tree,

Yellow-Shafted Flicker   Leonard Lee Rue III

I'm convinced a partridge would have put in an appearance, but they are sticking to the damp thickets this morning.

A trio of Canada jays, better and quite aptly known in the lumber camps as "camp robbers," arrive to accept the remnants of my breakfast. One, a dark-gray yearling, is especially bold, perching calmly at the edge of my table to await its due portion.

The drizzle becomes a steady downpour, driven by an equally steady wind. The canoe paddles holding the edges of the tarpaulen aloft above the table shiver but hold. Pockets of rainwater form in the loose concavities of the canopy and must be drained

Canada Jay   Len Rue Jr.

every few minutes, a procedure accomplished simply by poking the tarpaulen upwards from below.

The campfire sputters, hisses and dies.

A fat vole, its reddish-brown fur matted by the rain, trudges back and forth across the road on some dire mission, looking very much like a cigar with wheels. Back and forth, back and forth....

One thing must be said in praise of rain-soaked campsites: there are far fewer bugs.

* * *

Leonard Lee Rue III

The huge bull moose stands belly-deep in the steel gray water of Littlefield Pond, sheets of liquid cascading from its magnificent antlers as he raises his head to scan the shoreline. He sees me now and stares toward the tangle of marsh grass and sweetfern where I stand in the gentle rain. For a few indescribable moments, our eyes meet and our brains frantically weigh the situation. With a low bellow and a shake of his prodigious snout, he's off, churning the water behind him as he lurches with almost incongruous grace from the pond and vanishes into the maple and birch forest that rises along the flanks of Horse Mountain.

Almost as soon as the bull's wake has dissipated, a cow moose appears at the edge of the pond, shaking a hoof at the water's surface as if to test its consistency and temperature. She is wary, perhaps a bit unnerved by the sounds of the fleeing bull. She ventures slowly into the water but does not lower her head to yank the succulent roots and tubers from the muddy bottom. Instead, she merely stands for a few minutes in the drizzle before returning to the cloak of brush and trees.

Droplets of rainwater have collected in the open blossoms of the highbush blueberry that crowd a small knoll overlooking the pond. The bushes are thick and heavy with the blossoms, promising a healthy late-summer crop certain to attract the bears whose tracks I've followed up the trail in years past.

That trail, a gentle ribbon stretching a mile and a half through a high-canopied hardwood forest from the roadway, has become a veritable river by the time I turn my back on the pond. It gushes with cold water, coursing over the roots and rocks, undermining the bracken and infant maples. I take to the fern-carpeted edge of the trail and soon my pants are soaking from the droplet-laden leaves.

Again and again, the beech, poplar and maple trees send their watery burdens thundering to the forest floor, passing first over my foolishly unprotected head and shoulders as I lurch through the mud. The storm is a fortuitous event, however, for the yearling trout that cram the pools of the brook that parallels the trail: a cornucopia of insect food plummets into their domain from the rain-raked trees above and the fish dine with a ravenous frenzy.

I would estimate that most all American homes are located within what I call "the hum zone," where always there are the sounds of a mechanized society. Even in the outskirts of the most rural of communities there are human noises. The everpresent drone of giant tractor-trailer trucks on a highway three miles dis-

Common Loon — Leonard Lee Rue III

tant. The whine of a cottage or farm generator. The ticking of a watch.

One must go deep within the northwoods to truly escape "the hum zone." There, you may stand in a clearing among the mantled spruce and feel the wings of a nighthawk stir the air against your cheek.

Against the gathering dusk the nighthawk comes, on pointed, sharply jointed wings. Noiselessly, it banks in tightening circles over my campsite until it is within arm's reach, mouth agape to engulf the mosquitoes swarming about my head. As silently as it arrived, it is gone, a curious wraith of the evening and dawn.

I am no longer alone ... in human terms. Two young men have set up housekeeping in a seemingly cavernous department-store tent some one hundred yards to the east. Until now, I've been sharing life with other breeds of creatures, such as the cow moose who joined me at the outhouse this morning. I should have known then that it would be a "moose day."

She came snorting out of the brush on the opposite side of the roadway, probably from the cache of calcium chloride, and strolled into my campsite. Startled by the smoky campfire and scattered paraphernalia, she bolted straight up the path to the one-seater where I was serenely positioned, stopped a dozen feet from the open doorway and stared.

"Hmmm ... So that's how they do it," she seemed to think as she stood in the drizzle. Thus educated in the machinations of the human body, she strode calmly away.

The whippoorwill and loon are playing two-part harmony on the still night air. The loon, crying from one of the river's inaccessible backwaters, sounds almost gull-like in its "laughter," though I think its mood is far more serious than that of its distant cousin. Its chorus is, in many ways, to be felt rather than heard, as is the drumming of the male grouse.

From deep within the spruce hummocks between the roadway and the river I heard the drumming today. Muted somewhat by the drizzle and mist, it was nonetheless powerful, full of brute strength and earnest lust. A great moving of air, colliding between the compression of two widespread, anxious wings.

A wary rabbit emerges from the low dogwoods behind my tent, its dim form barely visible at the perimeter of light cast by my kerosene lantern. A spruce log crackles in the fire and the animal vanishes. Moving away from the fire and lantern, I stand in the roadway, listening to the nightsounds and straining my eyes to

White-tailed Deer Fawn   Irene Vandermolen

find their sources. A deer joins me, standing motionless and attentive two dozen yards away. We exchange stares for a few moments until it tires of my companionship and, tail lowered in a statement of ease, walks slowly into the darkness.

The river is running strong this morning, swelled by the constant rains of the past three days. Its surface swirls and boils as it rushes through the narrow gap once spanned by a bridge on the lumbering thoroughfare known as the "Burma Road." Now overgrown with alder and sweetfern, the road snakes eight miles from the opposite bank of the river to the confluence of two large streams, streams which in their merging become a river ocean-bound and doomed by the awaiting effluence of factories, mills and towns. At that frothy confluence eight miles distant, Henry David Thoreau found solace in the grace of the northwoods. He still could find it here.

Guy Gannett Publishing Co.

Barn and tree swallows swoop over the water and on the opposite bank a pileated woodpecker hammers on the sun-bleached skin of a dead elm. High above the watercourse, chimney swifts flutter in disjointed circles.

The river is too turbulent for solo canoeing. I'd have little trouble running from the bridge gap to the lake two miles to the east, but my lightweight aluminum canoe would be hard-pressed to buck the currents and deceptive eddies on the upstream return. I had so wanted to reach the tiny islands scattered about the lake where it is joined by the river, osprey-haunted oases visited by humans only on the rarest of occasions. The temptation to ignore the obvious hazards is great, but common sense must prevail.

Common sense dictates, also, that the time has come to turn homeward. The sun is trying to squeeze through the thick barrier of clouds and the rain has eased to a soft mist.

John Patriquin

MUD & STUFF

Dirt.

How often do we pause to consider how truly vital it is to life? I don't mean the filth of streets, playgrounds and sidewalks, but the honest dirt of forest, marsh and field that is called "soil" in those circles where it is respected, studied and even, sometimes, accorded a measure of reverence.

As above-ground creatures of some bulk, we tend to revel in the beauties and mysteries that most easily command our attention. A maple cloaked in brilliant red is difficult to ignore, but seldom do we ponder what lies beneath our feet, the smaller plants, miniscule animals, minerals and chemicals without which no maple and no human could survive.

The soil which covers all but a small portion of our world's surface is quite literally at the roots of our existence.

In the simplest of terms, soil is rock. Eons ago, long before the emergence of life, the infant oceans and ageless winds launched their ongoing conflict with the bedrock separating the planet's core from the void of space. Cataclysms wracked the bedrock from below.

What had been solid rock began to break down. Monstrous, wind-pushed waves hurled rock against rock. Small rocks became still smaller. Torrential rains and awesome tides drew rock across the barren land, grinding grit from bedrock. The grit began to collect in tenuously protected crevices and cracks.

And then occurred the ultimate of mysteries. Life blossomed; strange, one-celled organisms and algae populating the calming seas. The presence of life meant the presence of death and the remains of these miniscule organisms, borne by the wind and water, also settled into crevices and cracks.

The organic matter was the glue necessary to bind grit particle to grit particle and only with the meeting of the two was true soil produced. The foundation for all terrestrial life was laid.

The back forty is littered with rock, much of it cracked and broken by the immense pressure of the last glacier but all wreathed in vegetation. It is hardly coincidental that the trees and shrubs and ferns share such close quarters with the rocks and boulders.

An opaque tendril from a young maple's root stem squeezes into an imperceptible fracture along the surface of a large, buried

Guy Gannett Publishing Co.

boulder. A year passes... Two years... Three years... The tendril hardens and expands. Four years... In the muffled darkness of the earth, the boulder cracks under the strain. One of the boulder's halves bears a thin fracture into which a pliable tendril squeezes....

Above, the maturing maple sheds its cloak of leaves, scattering them at its feet where the debris of other plants and the bones, fur and feathers of countless animals collect in the "litter zone." It is here, in the musty dampness of nature's refuse, that an astonishing portion of the world's creatures find food, protection and the conditions in which to raise their young.

It is estimated that a single square meter of this fertile litter is

Isabel Lewando

home to as many as one billion creatures, from the one-celled organisms who put the whole process into motion to small mammals. Most are born here, sustain themselves on the litter or their fellow litter-lovers, expel rich wastes directly into the soil, aerate the material with their comings and goings, and ultimately give up their bodies to the earth.

Dust to dust; ashes to ashes. Soil to soil.

These inhabitants of the soil are exceptionally specialized: many of the smaller organisms are responsible for freeing carbon dioxide from the soil, thereby enabling plants to complete the photosynthetic process that provides the air we breathe.

The material contained in the litter zone is not true soil but, as the phrase implies, debris. The true soil lies below, where the debris has been chewed, digested, pulverized and otherwise broken down and compacted for untold years.

Until relatively recently, humankind took the world's soil pretty much for granted, using it with little or no consideration of the consequences of certain uses. The disasterous "Dust Bowl" of the 1930s Southwest was caused, to a very large degree, by excessive cultivation of the once rich soil. Farmers failed to take the precautions necessary to protect their acreage from wind and rain: wind first stripped the land of topsoil and rain then finished the job, gnawing huge, untillable gullies across the landscape.

The adoption of more conscientious farming methods has partially eliminated the likelihood of another such catastrophe, but care is and always will be absolutely critical in our treatment of the soil. And perhaps the most effective method of assuring that we are careful is to more completely understand and appreciate the pivotal role the soil plays in the maintenance of terrestrial life.

* * *

When I first came to live on the back forty, I hired a local woodcutter to fell a giant but regrettably dead elm tree that overshadowed the comparatively frail farmhouse.

The tree provided an ample quantity of long-burning firewood and a revealing glimpse into its past, a glimpse articulated by its 150 rings. Each of a tree's rings represents a single year of its life and is an eloquent statement of the conditions it faced during the growing phase of that year, a spokesman for the natural and unnatural elements.

A tree's trunk is comprised of four layers. The outermost is the bark, affording protection from the elements and the insects. Inside the bark lies the phloem or inner bark, carrying food manufactured by the leaves to other parts of the tree. Next comes the cambium and, finally, the xylem or wood, the latter containing two sublayers, the sapwood and the heartwood.

It is the cambium which holds the key to tree growth. Using sugars produced by the leaves, the cambium manufactures new tissue, therewith adding to the bulk and the girth of the tree. The tissue manufactured by the cambium forms rings, rather like the ripples created when a stone is cast into a pool of calm water ... except that these rings "ripple" inward. The rings live for several years before becoming so permeated with resin, oil, tannin

Guy Gannett Publishing Co.

Bob Niss

and other substances that they die. These innermost rings, now part of the heartwood, lend valuable support to the entire tree, thus assuring its survival.

The heartwood is often easily detected because its quantity of tannins and resins leaves it a darker color than the outer growth. Sometimes, insects or their larvae gain access to the heartwood and ultimately cause the tree to fall by robbing it of the supportive backbone of wood. Cracks caused by lightning or improper pruning may provide the means of access, not only for insects but for fungae, mosses and other equally destructive opportunists.

Scientists are examining tree rings with increasing attentiveness, most notably those of the bristlecone pine of Nevada which, at nearly 5,000 years of age, is the oldest known variety of tree in the world. Such ancient trees have become invaluable in the dating of certain archeological sites, confirming or altering chrono-

Allan Swenson

logical data acquired by other, sometimes questionable means.

It is rather breathtaking to think that there are trees living today which sprouted before the Egyptian Empire had been solidified. It is nearly as breathtaking to consider what our backyard trees can tell us about the days prior to our arrival.

Generally speaking, the thickness of a tree's rings mirrors the climatic conditions at the time they were produced. A thin ring represents a year in which tissue production was slowed, the most common cause being below-normal resources of water.

The presence of several particularly thin rings in succession often means an extended drought occurred at that point in a tree's life. Archeologists puzzling over the sudden and apparently inexplicable abandonment of an old Indian community site may well turn to the rings of surviving or preserved trees in an attempt to solve the riddle: a succession of thin rings coinciding with the

Guy Gannett Publishing Co.

time of abandonment could mean that a drought forced the inhabitants to seek greener pastures.

But there are countless other factors involved in the production and the thickness of tree rings.

A thin ring may also be the result of forest overcrowding. When trees overpopulate a given area, each must compete for a generally limited supply of water and light. All are less able to manufacture normal quantities of food and tissue. Such periods of overcrowding may continue for decades, ended only by disease, fire or human intervention. Partial thinning of a crowded forest may produce uneven rings, thicker on the less crowded side than on that where competition persists.

Successively thin rings may also reflect a period of disease or insect infestation. The larvae of many insects dine gluttonously on the leaves and needles of trees, decreasing as surely as drought their ability to maintain previous tissue production rates. Anything which adversely affects a tree's food and tissue production is ultimately echoed in the thickness of its rings.

Thick rings, on the other hand, most always echo times of plenty, when warmth, sunlight, water, air and the proper combination of minerals accelerated a tree's growth. Like their thin relatives, thick rings may also be caused by a variety of factors that have little or nothing to do with nutrition and the atmosphere.

A tree whose rings are punctuated by burn scars may reveal a series of thin rings immediately succeeding those scars, followed by a succession of thick rings. Such a configuration would indicate that the tree struggled briefly after a fire ravaged the forest and then flourished as its more seriously damaged former competitors crumbled to ashen dust.

* * *

"I forgot," Matt said quickly.

"I didn't know she was cleaning," whispered Josh.

My two sons stood at the edge of the small pond with a wagon brimming with "perfect skippers" just after having tromped through the kitchen and living room in mud-caked sneakers, right past Judy who was cleaning the two rooms ... for the second time in 24 hours.

"Okay, guys. It's mud season, all right, but that's no reason to be slobs. How'd you like it if you'd just tidied up your rooms and I came in and just threw everything back on the floor?"

I reminded them that the farmhouse is equipped with "a gen-

Guy Gannett Publishing Co.

uine mudroom where we're supposed to take off our muddy things." I don't believe they had ever really stopped to think about the connection between the little hallway and the stuff on their boots.

Mudrooms. Like hoop rolling and sleigh riding, they've slipped into yesterday, forgotten by all but the eldest of our elders. (My mother will no doubt bridle at that phrase, relate vivid tales about all three and then solemnly note that she is "hardly old enough to be the eldest of anyone's elders!")

Even when I was a kid — not very long ago, of course — the mudroom was a thing of the past, a mysterious place where I assumed great mountains of mud reposed, oozing beneath the doorway to threaten unsuspecting children with slimy, agonizing suffocation. Visions of "the mudroom that ate the Niss kid" plagued me for years.

I certainly know better now. Mudrooms are functional little places. Messy, but functional. Ours lies in ambush between the garage and the kitchen and can be avoided only when the front door is in use, or about once a year. It's about the size of a double bed, an astonishing fact when one stops to calculate its appetite for anything that dares to challenge its formidable gauntlet of coathooks and corners.

In the wintertime, it can accommodate 12 coats, seven vests, 43 mittens, 93 feet of rope, 19 and one-half knit hats, a dozen boots, 17 ice-covered socks, three hockey sticks, two snowsuits, two tool boxes, one day pack, 15 Matchbox cars and several cubic feet of snow, ice and dirt. That is, it will hold all that until someone gets so fed up with using compass and machete to get through that they threaten to toss in a stick of dynamite. When that happens, the room suddenly becomes larger and tidier.

Repulsive as it may be at times, I imagine it must have been far worse during its heyday, back when a mudroom was a *mud* room. That was when wagons, buggies and coaches rattled and groaned past the house on a twisting dirt road, pausing occasionally to let their horses and oxen refresh themselves at the stone trough that then stood by the roadside. The pastures, kitchen garden, stables and paths to the barn, well and woodshed no doubt provided ample quantities of dirt, grime and muck, too.

I sometimes think I can hear the faint echoes of life in the farmhouse as it was then, a century or more ago. Some of the echoes are unfamiliar, others as clear as the noises of today.

"Take those boots off before you come in here! What do you think the mudroom is for?"

Guy Gannett Publishing Co.

VISIONS

Anesthetized by visions of our own perfection, we cannot accept it. We hear the whispered hints and see the veiled evidence, but always the self-imposed boundaries of our own senses deny the final revelation.

We are but one of countless tribes of Earth tenants, peers aboard one of billions of galactic islands. Henry Beston called them "nations."

The tenant tribes are diverse, and in that diversity we find the solace of our superiority. We are superior by standards we impose. We write encyclopedias, compose music, build cities and ponder the cosmos. Always, though, our ponderings and our constructions reflect the limitations of our tribe.

Are our symphonies more perfect than a whalesong because we have "mastered" the construction and use of instruments? We mistake preference for perfection. Our human ears prefer the human symphony; the whale prefers the whalesong. The whale, of course, has no need of instruments and our subtle conclusion is that it, therefore, is a "lesser" creature. The whale, on the other hand, may consider ours the "lesser" of the tribes, reliant as our music is on the inanimate objects we call instruments.

The whale has no such conceptions because it cannot reason, we say. We say, in languages which themselves are considered proof of our superiority, dialects comprised of sounds — noises, if you will — that are hardly a monopoly of our tribe. Our vocal range is far more restricted, in fact, than that of countless other tribes and often less precisely structured.

We are only beginning to realize that other tenant tribes have languages, too. Burdened by our sense of superiority, we ponder how best to "use" the communicative tribes. We "educate" them, blessing them with such skills as the ability to jump through hoops or retrieve lost military hardware.

What do they think about it, I wonder. Do they find us laughable in our ignorance? Are they saddened by their subservience? Are they angry?

But they cannot "think," we insist, proving our point again with standards developed by one tribe to evaluate another. We forget how unsuccessful our efforts have been to evaluate our own tribe's various clans. We exterminated the Mayans because they were "barbaric," only to learn centuries later that they had a social, religious and economic system the equal of their executioner's. Dif-

John Snow

ferent, yes, and perhaps barbaric by "civilized" standards, but not "lower" and certainly not worthy of extinction.

The human tribe is a newcomer, an infant compared to the vast majority of its neighbor tribes. We have evolved, whether by divine grace or natural selection, more rapidly than the other tribes. But rapidity and superiority are not necessarily synonymous.

Like the limbs of a giant tree, the Earth's tribes have developed at different rates and times and in different shapes, heeding the dictates of the tree's surroundings. The oldest and the youngest limbs are both the strongest and the weakest. The oldest are strong in experience, weak in their susceptibility to dramatic change. The youngest find strength in supple exuberance and weakness in inexperience.

The eldest of the Earth's tribes have been the least able to cope with the dramatic changes precipitated by the exuberant, inexperienced human tribe, and yet they may prove more enduring. The meek may indeed inherit the Earth, overcoming the ultimate human tragedy with patient experience. They have, after all, weathered the cataclysms of eons, learning at each turn in the path, storing and refining their knowledge in libraries we cannot or will not enter, writing encyclopedias with inks we cannot see.

We are nonetheless doing all we can to burn their libraries. Sadly, we hold the torch to their books with hardly a glimpse at their contents.

The din of our ships' engines has all but drowned the whalesong, splintering in less than two centuries a communications network that had spanned the entire globe for unknown eons. We, whose global communications network is infantile and rudimentary by comparison, are beginning to understand the complexity and extent of the leviathans' tribal network, just as we now have an inkling of the complexity and extent of the Mayan civilization. Understanding and appreciation can be two very different propositions.

On land, we marvel at the order of the beehive or the anthill and sometimes call their occupants "social" creatures. Our tribute is condescending and tainted by the belief that they are "blind" or "instinctive" in their obedience to that order. Is their blindness any different from our unyielding images of them, or from our notions of our own social order and its supremacy?

We see the same blind obedience in the migration of birds and are awed by their feats of endurance, strength and perception. We, too, migrate, but we must be borne north and south in the bowels of metal machines whose mortality rates may be greater

Maine Fish & Game Dept.

than that of the goose.

We are flabbergasted to find that chimpanzees and even some birds actually use tools, digging for grubs or weaving nests with expertly wielded sticks. The use of tools, after all, is a uniquely human trait, so we conclude that non-human users of tools are oddities among their tribes, quirks of adaptive instinct. Is it not possible that a reliance on tools is a weakness or liability? Needless to say, we do not think so.

We do not stop to think that maybe — just maybe — we are simply unable to detect the faint echo of something more, something that defies our religious and scientific perceptions of order, evolution and grace.

We anxiously await — and fear — the discovery of "intelligent life" elsewhere in the cosmos. Our search sends computers hur-

Gordon Chibroski

tling silently through space and points giant antennae toward unseen, pulsing lights. Our search is sanctioned by the conviction that ours is the only intelligent tribe on this mote of galactic dust, a tribe that can catalogue the composition of stars and comets.

We have not yet begun to catalogue the composition of a whale-song, self-certain that the "dominion" we enjoy over the "great whales and every living creature that moveth" means absolute control without absolute understanding. The sovereign who does not understand his people is likely to feel his throne tremble after a moment or two of gluttony.

We forget that in both Biblical and evolutionary terms, the human tribe is but a moment old, an after-thought of sorts. Poised on the brink of revelation, we withdraw unto ourselves and plunge with the greatest blindness of all down a path that leads to....

Guy Gannett Publishing Co.

ON TOWARD SUMMER

It dropped with a soft "plop" onto the surface of the pond beneath the maple tree. Only its head punctured the surface and, tail and hind legs depressing the tenacious film, it struggled to reach the safety of the bottom.

It was a rare sight, one seldom seen by daylight-loving humans. A salamander was making the momentous transition from terrestrial to aquatic life . . . and it was in dire trouble. Had the pond contained fish or had its frogs been more alert, the salamander would have disappeared very quickly, but a gentle prod from a long stick sent the amphibian plummeting to its new home amid the rocks and decaying leaves three feet below.

The salamander's dive itself was somewhat unusual. Not known for its tree-climbing abilities, it nonetheless elected to enter the water from a limb seven feet above the surface and about five feet from the trunk which it had to have scaled to reach the base of the limb. The time-consuming ascent had obviously robbed the salamander's skin of considerable moisture, leaving it too dry to simply slip through the surface film encasing the pond.

I wonder. Had the salamander tried unsuccessfully to enter the water from land and opted for the dive because its skin was drying? (Salamanders sometimes live in trees that have water-holding cavities, but the tree from which it dove had no such refuges and I, therefore, must assume the climb was undertaken with the dive in mind.) Is a salamander capable of such problem-solving?

Mysteries abound in the back forty. And the salamander is one of its most mysterious inhabitants.

It is a creature of great variety and geographical distribution. There are more than 300 species in the world, ranging in length from a couple of inches to a whopping five feet (in the case of the appropriately-named giant salamander of Japan that sometimes lives for more than a century) and in coloration from basic brown to brilliant orange and red.

With few exceptions, all salamanders pass through an aquatic stage in their lives, generally as larvae that closely resemble the tadpole young of frogs and toads. Even in their terrestrial stages, they require considerable moisture to keep their skin and glands functioning and therefore seldom venture from their damp havens beneath logs, rocks or leaves during the daylight hours.

Despite superficial similarities, salamanders and lizards are not

Red Eft Maine Fish & Game Dept.

related: the former are amphibians with smooth, moist skin while the latter are scale-covered reptiles. The frog is the salamander's closest relative.

The most familiar North American salamander is the red-spotted newt of our Eastern ponds, a four-inch creature with a confusing and rather atypical life profile. In its larval stage, it is aquatic. As a juvenile, it is terrestrial, easily identified by its red-orange skin punctuated by small, orderly spots of brighter red, and is commonly known as a red eft. As an adult, it reverts to its aquatic ways, trades its red-orange skin for green and retains its orderly spots of red.

It was a red eft, or juvenile red-spotted newt, that dove into the back forty pond.

Almost as familiar to New Englanders is the spotted salamander, a larger and fatter creature distinguished by dark, yellow-spotted skin from which it can secrete a cloudy liquid if improperly handled or threatened. Unlike the red-spotted newt, it spends its adulthood on land, though it also needs ample moisture in order to survive.

While most salamanders spend the winter months hibernating

Spotted Salamanders   Leonard Lee Rue III

beneath rotting logs, deep within stone walls or buried in pond muck, some — most notably the spotted salamander — turn up in the cellars and crawl spaces of older homes and may hibernate only lightly, facing the perils posed by cats, mice and misunderstanding humans.

Just as the salamander's life is among the most varied in the animal kingdom, so its diet is among the most diverse. As aquatic larvae or adults they dine on a wealth of insects, including mosquito larvae, and such delicacies as leeches, worms, frogs' eggs and tadpoles. As terrestrial creatures they favor terrestrial insects, worms, caterpillars and, in some cases, carrion.

Perhaps the most curious and enviable quality of the salamander is its ability to grow new legs or a new tail if the original equipment is severed by predators or otherwise amputated. It is an expert in the art and consequently is the object of considerable laboratory scrutiny. Maybe the salamander will someday enable us to do likewise.

But don't look to it for diving lessons.

* * *

Guy Gannett Publishing Co.

To build or not to build? That is the question.

Ever since my father erected a magnificent cedar cabin "playhouse" in our backyard, I've had a passion for the rustic structures, though the roots of my passion change.

As a freshman in college, several friends and I dreamed of grabbing a chunk of tax delinquent land in the nearby Rocky Mountains and building a retreat for the fulfillment of other, baser dreams.

And now, living on the flanks of a woodlot with plenty of on-the-spot building materials, the dream returns. But the dream is haunted by the specter of the tax man and building code officer. I can see it now.

"I see you've made some improvements here, Mr. Niss. Let's see ... that bridge across the stream certainly does boost your market value and, by the way, you didn't get the proper permit ... er, No. 47-A, I believe. And that bridge certainly does not have the required cross-overbuck stress lock munchkin or handrail rest-o-knuckle flapdoodle. Where is the weight limit designation?"

"But, it's only a couple of logs and a half-dozen old planks!"

"Wait just a taxable minute, Mr. Niss! Is that a dwelling over there in the woods?"

"Well, no. Not really. It's just a little 12-by-12 shack I put together one weekend. Sort of a hideaway, if you know what I mean."

"I most definitely do, Mr. Niss. You've hidden it away all right. I can find no reference to it on my tax list, so I must assume it is not in compliance with Code 498, Chapter 23, Subtitle L-2.7, Clause 224.

"You may be able to get an after-the-fact variance, but I'll have to file a report on its septic system, wiring, plumbing and footings. May I see the blueprints, percolation statistics and leaching field specifications?"

"But . . . I think I'll just burn it down. Would that take care of things?"

"Provided you have a burning permit."

Technically speaking, the simplest of cabins can be regarded as an "improvement" to one's property, subject to all the ordinances, zoning restrictions, setback requirements, property tax schedules and other red tape that a municipality can unleash. They can't be ignored.

Well, they can, but he who builds anything without checking

first with everyone else is asking for trouble; things like fines, back taxes and interest penalties, not to mention the possibility of being told to take one giant step backward, aided by a bulldozer.

But if the woodlot owner can somehow decipher and cope with the do's and don'ts, a simple cabin can indeed be a glorious thing, whether employed as a refuge from domestic chaos, a working retreat for the artist or writer or as a guest house for frazzled visitors from the urban jungles.

It can be an "improvement" in more than technical, taxable terms.

Intelligently built and properly maintained, a woodlot cabin will boost the market value of that woodlot and whatever other structures it contains. One could even get a bit mercenary about it, hawking the property package with the clinching enticement that "its canopy of pine and birch hides a rustic, tranquil cabin designed with the lover of nature and solitude in mind."

The question goes unanswered. Perhaps I'll dig a cave. Then again, I'd probably need an excavator's license or an archeological permit.

Dreams and reality have a way of meshing, contrary as they may seem. The dream of a secluded cabin meshes and flickers in the shadow of the barn, a demanding reality that also embraces dreams... and ghosts. Unfortunately, the reality of the barn is all too demanding.

Rising like a great, seedy battleship from the ledge east of the farmhouse, the barn has been gathering dust, mildew, rat skeletons, domestic debris and scrap lumber for decades and the stuff has to be dealt with before the barn itself suffers. It isn't the most delightful of tasks, but it must be done.

Pushing valiantly through a haze of dusty cobwebs, I managed to completely clean one end of the second floor last weekend. That leaves about four and two-thirds floors to go, counting the below-ground "dungeon." With the exception of that dank and foreboding floor, each at one time housed chickens. Anyone who has lived on a farm knows what that means: a thick layer of foul fowl droppings to scrape from beams, floors and window sills.

Like I said, it isn't the most delightful of tasks.

A barn, like a house, requires care. It requires paint, nails, putty, glass, shingles, bolts and boards... and no small amount of sweat and money. Those left too long to their own devices require substantial amounts of the latter if they are to survive and anyone

John Patriquin

considering the purchase of a farmstead that includes a barn should take that fact into careful consideration. "Rustic," the term often used to describe a country barn, all too often means dilapidated.

Because barns tend to serve as closets for the owners' discards, the opening of a barn door is akin to the opening of a window on its owners' lives. There, reposing in the dust and shadows, are whispers of human desires, disappointments, joys and struggles: a box of cancelled checks, a splintered sled, yellowed school photographs, broken canning jars, a bottle of cheap perfume, letters, melted crayons, a glassless aquarium, mildewed clothes, a bedpan.

Barns are never really cleaned. They are adjusted. Every few decades, a new owner or new generation substitutes his discards for those of his predecessors, pausing only long enough to wonder why such things were saved as they are crammed into boxes and bags for the trip to the landfill.

Once the cleaning — er, adjusting — is done, the barn's true health comes to light. It is often only then that the owner fully appreciates the responsibilities inherent in barn ownership.

The beams and braces in the corner where 16 dresses, nine coats, 13 pairs of pants and one girdle were heaped need reinforcement. That box of jars hid a large crack in the wall and the woodwork has become rotted by rain and snow. Water also apparently crept in through the cracks in a window hidden for untold years behind a half-dozen bales of wood chips.

Those barns which have been used to house birds and beasts pose additional problems. They can be genuinely repulsive places, filled with the droppings of the domestic animals and the droppings, nests and remains of the vermin they attracted. Moisture creeps in and does it work, aided and accelerated by the chemicals in the animal droppings. The decay and the odor attract insects which attract spiders which fill every crevice and corner with thick webs which trap dust which holds moisture which accelerates the rot which . . .

Clapboards and shingles become loose. Window frames decay. Doors tilt. Floors warp. Glass cracks. Stairs buckle.

Thankfully, barns need not be kept as pristine as houses. There is a difference between pristine and solid. Whereas a house needs glass in its windows, a barn can get by with heavy-gauge plastic. Not many folks would cover a traffic-gouged kitchen floor with unadorned plywood, but that will do admirably in a hoof-scarred, water-warped barn. Bent-over nails will hold barn windows in place but are hardly acceptable in houses. Scrap lumber, leftover

John Patriquin

paint, odd shingles, discarded hardware and other scrounged materials can turn a doomed barn into a rejuvenated, reasonably solid structure.

The process of rejuvenating an old barn can also be somewhat financially profitable, though probably not sufficiently so to pay for the job. Old windows, bed frames, hardware, copper wiring and piping, books, clothing, tools, motors, feed bins, jars, suitcases and other paraphernalia will demand a few bucks on the barn sale market.

Anyone want to buy a nice bedpan? Only 50 cents.

And then, a few decades from now, someone else can weed through your discards as they tackle the next several generations of cobwebs and dust, muttering all the while about the worthless debris some folks accumulate.

* * *

I have been accused on more than one occasion of carrying on outlandish love affairs with all the elements of the outdoors. "You like everything that moves out there and most things that don't," one friend charged, noting that the objects of my affection include bats, leeches, rats and coyotes.

That's not entirely true.

When it comes to the mosquito, I have a hard time figuring out just where it fits into the scheme of things, the delicate chain of life. And because my affection for living things is very much dictated by their supportive relationships to other living things, I find it just beyond my usually tolerant capabilities to like the beast.

The mosquito is relished by a number of birds, including swallows, flycatchers, whippoorwills and nighthawks, a fact which would seem to give it some redeeming function. But the puzzle is that these and other birds — and certainly humans — could get along quite well without the mosquito: just when the insect is at its most ravenously populous level, countless other, meatier insects are similarly plentiful.

It is quite likely that some "early birds," appearing before the bulk of our native insects have matured, are saved from starvation by the frequently premature mosquito. It is also likely that Adolf Hitler at one time performed a good deed.

Another argument on behalf of the mosquito's stature as an integral link in the chain of life is the fact that it, like all creatures, is host to a variety of parasites, some of which survive only in association with a specific kind of mosquito. The utter extermination of

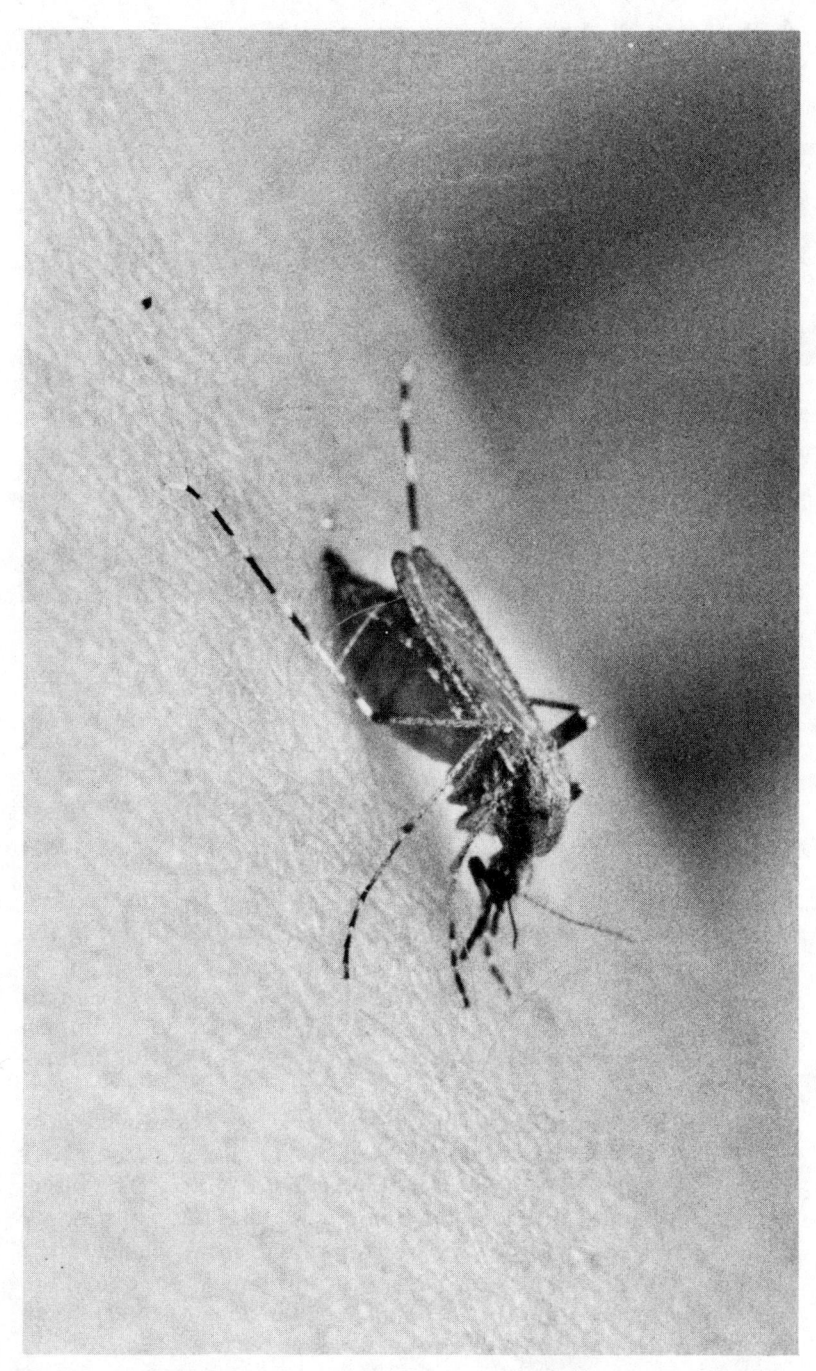

Mosquito   John Snow

Green Dragonfly   Leonard Lee Rue III

the mosquito, some purists argue, would herald the simultaneous extinction of these other living creatures, inconsequential in human terms but bound one to another with a complexity we may never understand.

We've wiped out the greak auk, the dodo, the passenger pigeon and probably the ivory-billed woodpecker without ruining civilization, so what harm can be done if a similar fate is allotted the lowly mosquito?

No one knows. It may be generations before the loss of a single species exerts its full influence on the "chain of life," so it is impossible to say "yea" or "nay" to the mosquito . . . or to the Furbish lousewart or the snail darter.

But the problem of mosquito control persists, enlivened by the "need" for biteless barbecues and placid picnics, and the East's countless back forties are typical mosquito country. The biters breed in sinkholes, marshes, bogs, ponds and ditches, but they are by no means restricted to such watery environs. A winged adult can travel several miles in a single day and may appear, much to the chagrin of the uninitiated, on an ocean beach or island, mountaintop or deep within a dry forest.

For too many years we've sprayed and dusted the insect with an array of chemicals whose properties and perils are only now becoming obvious. We have managed to create "super mosquitoes" as resistant to chemical warfare as a bobcat is to a salamander attack. We are just starting to accept the fact that the ingredients of this chemical warfare, used with such abandon for so many years, do not merely disappear. They wind up in our drinking water, livestock, produce and in the very tissues and bones that are our physical framework and essence.

Alternatives are being explored. Dragonfly nymphs and adults are being stocked in especially mosquito-laden areas. Cannibalistic mosquitoes are being bred and stocked. And chemicals have not been altogether disregarded as weapons: there is still hope that a compound can be developed which affects only mosquitoes and dissipates shortly after use without posing unseen hazards.

The dragonfly option seems a step in the right direction, one whose ultimate success hinges entirely on the quite natural fact that dragonflies seem almost to drool at the prospect of a mosquito feast. It is a natural enemy of the mosquito, but it is not alone. Indeed, the most voracious of the mosquito's foes may be the equally maligned bat, a creature that is hardly in short supply in most temperate regions.

The bats are among the most ancient of animals, strangely twittering creatures of the night that first stretched their leathery wings some 55 million years ago. Today there are an estimated 900 species of bats inhabiting all but the very coldest regions of the world. As devotees of darkness, they do not quite fit into the human "scheme of things" and we find them strange, threatening and not a little evil.

To most people, "bat" means "vampire," but the true vampire bat is Latin American rather than Transylvanian and hardly the menace of film and fantasy. It does subsist on blood, its throat being too narrow to accommodate anything but liquids, and occasionally laps (but cannot suck) blood from human wounds.

The bats of the back forty, however, are essentially harmless creatures. They are no more likely to become entangled in one's hair than is a bird or dragonfly and their appearance in one's attic has nothing to do with impending disaster. The back forty bats, such as the hoary and little brown bats, are among the smaller of the world's diversely constructed bats with bodies about four inches long and wingspreads seldom exceeding a foot. That's a far cry from the "flying fox" of Southeast Asia, a giant that weighs as much as two and a half pounds and may have a wingspread of five feet, not much less than that of a young eagle.

Bats are phenomenal aerialists, blessed with an echo-location or "radar" system that can successfully guide a blinded individual across a room criss-crossed by intertwining string. Their aerial talents are further boosted by highly flexible wings consisting of two layers of skin stretched across their forelimbs and long "finger" bones. Most bats have a third "wing," a slim tail connected to their trailing legs with thin but strong flaps of skin. Both tail and wings are frequently used to trap insects in mid-air, much as a baseball shortstop scoops up ground balls with a fluid, sweeping motion of his glove.

Bats are unique in that they are the only mammals that can truly fly — "flying" squirrels merely glide — but they are in no way close kin of the birds. They are such highly developed and specialized flyers, in fact, that they are virtually incapable of walking: like birds but unlike humans, their legs bend backward at the knee. Birds have learned to hop and some have even forsaken the air for terrestrial lifestyles, but bats can only fold their wings about their bodies and pull themselves forward with limbs not meant for such tasks.

There is no denying the fact that bats are downright ugly, but the bulbous, pig-like noses of some and the long, vein-lined ears of others are the utterly indispensible products of highly selective evolution. A bat's ears are the equivalent of a human's eyes, retreiving its orally emitted and humanly inaudible "radar" signals and telling its brain precisely what is in its flight path, from trees to gnats. Just as our eyes dictate the actions of our feet, so a bat's ears communicate directly with its wings.

Except for a handful of species that are not found in this neck of the woods, bats are entirely nocturnal, spending their days hanging upside-down in barns, sheds, eaves, garages, attics and hollow trees. The greatest concentrations of bats, however, can be found in deep, constantly cool caverns, some of which may house millions of individuals. While spelunking in Colorado several years ago, I came across a cavern whose entire roof was hidden by roosting bats. The floor of the cavern was buried to a depth of about two feet by their droppings and remains, the latter picked clean by a squirming horde of beetles and worms. It was not the most pleasant place I've visited.

While bats are admittedly ugly and untidy, they are among the most voracious and efficient insect-eaters and their droppings make exceptionally good plant fertilizer. Some species even perform the bee-like task of pollinating flowers. Those factors should be considered before completely enclosing a barn, shed or other outbuilding where bats are known to roost. By all means, bat-proof your house and garage, but if you detest mosquitoes and the like you will find a firm ally in the bat.

The obvious intent of bat-proofing a building is to make it unaccessible to the animal, meaning that all cracks, holes and crevices must be closed. Like mice, bats can squeeze through the smallest of openings and even a hole left unplugged after a house has been filled with blown-in insulation is akin to an open barn door.

Strong, fine-mesh screening such as that used for windows and doors is ideal for closing most cracks, especially vents that must continue to serve their purpose. Missing window panes certainly must be replaced and doors that don't quite close should be repaired.

They may still find a way inside, in which case the best recourse is to constantly remind yourself that they are not the ogres we long have thought them to be. Unless you have a truly huge and growing colony of them or have a genuine love for mosquitoes and other insect pests, let them be.

* * *

A brown creeper hitches its way up one side of a pin cherry while a nuthatch clambers down the opposite side. A gray squirrel leaps from the ground to the sun-dappled trunk of an oak within which a flying squirrel sleepily awaits nightfall.

Amazing. Not that the flying squirrel is sleeping or that the creeper is creeping, but that it all fits so smoothly. We tend to call it "the scheme of things" or "God's design." Both are accurate.

If the creeper were to consistently descend rather than climb trees, it would become a direct competitor to the nuthatch in the search for bark-hiding insects. But as things are, the creeper is likely to dine on insects visible from below, the nuthatch on those which can be detected from above.

The two squirrels are kept from direct competition by the clear demarcation of night and day and by the added assurance that the flyer is unlikely to leave the trees that provide sufficient elevation for its glide launches.

A water snake lunges from a mid-pond log to snatch a young bullfrog while, a few dozen feet away in the cool grass of a field, a leopard frog vanishes into the maw of a garter snake. A mouse scurries noisily through a brush pile; below, a sightless mole ex-

Grey Squirrel Allan Swenson

White-Breasted Nuthatch   Leonard Lee Rue III

tends its tunnel through the perpetual darkness of the earth.

"The scheme of things." "God's design."

Call it what you will. I call it perfection, this maintenance of the thin line between coexistence and competition. The line holds. The creatures flourish.

Certainly, many creatures have strong competitors for their preferred food, but even between apparently competitive animals the strife is likely to be superficial. Do fly maggots and vultures really compete for the carcass of a deer?

Consider the leech in its many varieties, a "blood-sucker" whose competition with its kin would seem certain and incessant. But leeches inhabiting the same pond often have very different tastes: one variety seeks out turtles, another frogs, a third mammals and still another — one that can hardly be called a BLOOD-sucker — dines exclusively on the liquids to be found in plant stems.

Phoebe Leonard Lee Rue III

The term "flycatcher" would seem to reflect direct competition among those diminutive birds, but watch. The common phoebe darts from a bridge girder to snatch a moth fluttering inches above the stream below. The impressive crested flycatcher perches atop the tallest dead pine in the midst of a nearby swamp, scanning the damp air 50 feet above the water for larger prey. And the alder flycatcher flits among the bushes, snatching tiny insects from their leaves.

Just as the frogs on which the garter and water snakes feed have their own clearly defined, minimally competitive territories and eating habits, so the insects eaten by both the frogs and the flycatchers have built-in assurances of specialization that prevent undue competition.

Flies are notorious for their ecstasy at the sight of a dead animal, but some will have nothing to do with such rancid fare, preferring decaying vegetable matter or even the rotting remains of very specific kinds of plants. Some adult flies, in fact, never eat, their brief adulthood being devoted entirely to the process of reproduction.

The specialization — and hence the lack of competition — among insect larvae is nothing short of astonishing. Even on or within the leaves of a single plant, the larvae of several kinds of insects may dine on very different fare. And it is possible that the bodies of a few contain the parasitic larvae of other insects, tiny worms that instinctively avoid their hosts' vital organs until the very end.

Appearances are deceiving. What seems to be an utterly random search for food is anything but random. There is purpose and limitation and hence far less competition than one might believe. Above all, there is much to astonish and bewilder the human observer, especially he who ponders his own place within that careful, perplexing order.

Guy Gannett Publishing Co.

SUMMER

Red Fox Kits — Leonard Lee Rue III

NEW CHORDS

The woods are lush and filled with the exuberance of summer.

Gone with the damp warmth of spring are the hordes of mosquitoes and black flies. Erased is the expectant hush of nesting-time.

The field and forest tremble with a cacaphony of sounds and a blur of motion, the things of which midsummer daydreams are made.

The deer have vanished into the thickets and swamps, tending their young and venturing into the open woods only with the utmost caution. They have left no tracks in the soft earth ringing the ponds and along the logging road for nearly three weeks, though I suspect they have not been entirely absent.

A different matter altogether are the deer flies. Deer or no deer, they are present in excruciating numbers, buzzing constantly about the head and shoulders of anyone who ventures into the woods. A beard and long hair help somewhat, but neither they nor liberal applications of repellent can really keep the insects away. Their buzzing refrain is part of the midsummer symphony, though a part without which the composition would hardly suffer.

The blossoms of spring and early summer — the mayflowers, strawberries, lady's slippers and cranberry — have long wilted, dried and gone to seed, followed by the daylilies, milkweed, daisies and jewelweed. The burdocks are belly-high, their stalks and branches tipped by the purple-green flowers that soon will harden into the sticky burs whose sole purpose in life seems to be to cling to the coats of such domestic creatures as dogs, cats and children.

Dragonflies are everywhere, careening above the weed-filled ponds, snapping up the last brigades of mosquitoes and other small insects. They have been joined in the air by the first of the monarch butterflies, back from their wintering grounds far to the south in search of the milkweed on which to deposit their eggs.

Brown male gypsy moths bounce through the woodland shadows, seeking out the white females pressed against the tree trunks and rocks, heavy with eggs. There seem to be fewer of the moths this year than last: perhaps the population of their leaf-loving young will be similarly smaller next summer.

The sparrow hawks are trying to entice their young from the barn eaves, berating the innocents with raucous cries and threatening swoops. The robin's nest in the hydrangea at one corner of the farmhouse is fairly bursting with new feathers and beaks. A

Guy Gannett Publishing Co.

Toads — Isabel Lewando

pair of hummingbirds is nesting somewhere in the alders at the edge of the stream and they come daily to the nectar-filled feeder by the kitchen window, enthralling the kids with their speed and acrobatic maneuvers.

In the ponds, the tadpoles are no longer black dots against the embracing brown: they have fattened and are sprouting legs. Their parents croak deeply in the ranks of weeds, lunging forth now and then to "shoot" an errant fly, moth or beetle with their long, quick tongues.

Snakes are everywhere; garters, milk snakes, dainty ring-necks, hefty water snakes and camouflaged green snakes. They come to the old elm stump and the crevices between the granite blocks of the barn ramp to shed, leaving their opaque skins to wave in the warm breezes.

The midsummer daydream has begun, dappling the soul with its glow and its warmth.

* * *

Guy Gannett Publishing Co.

The back forty has no ocean frontage, but the ocean is part of all New Englanders. Those of us who choose to live away from the swell and the breakers need only to return to the seaside once in a while to renew the very special relationship.

The human soul is drawn to the sea as birds are drawn to the air. Those who embrace the precepts of evolution say the attraction is a vestige of our infancy, a response to whispers from our collective womb. Those who believe in the Biblical account of creation say the attraction is rooted in such divine acts as The Flood.

Whether by divine or circumstantial act, the seas and their inhabitants preceded us on this rock.

Standing at the tip of Estes Head in Eastport, battered by fierce winds and spattered by the droppings of countless wheeling gulls, one feels the sea. Not sees, but *feels*. It breathes and boils, wails and moans. It is a thing alive, the ultimate mystery and the key to all that was and is and will be.

I have never heard a whale, but the recordings of their "songs" that I have heard suggest theirs are the voices of the sea, vocal echoes of its heartbeat rolling across the miles and the eons. I could feel whalesongs there at Estes Head, as one senses the presence of another in a darkened room.

I have stood on more southerly beaches in the midst of hurricanes and ridden the ocean swell beyond the sight of land, but I have never felt as awed by the sea as when I faced it from Estes Head, and later from the shores of Cobscook Bay. There, far from the gentle tourist beaches of Cape Cod and Old Orchard, the sea runs with ecstatic strength and beauty. The Eastport-Cobscook Bay tides of 20 feet and more make Buzzards Bay and Casco Bay seem meek, for tides of such magnitude are powerful beyond imagination, immune from adequate description. Entire, seemingly bottomless bays are utterly emptied, their fish and seals riding the buoy-bending current to what must be truly bottomless waters.

Federal bureaucrats and elected desk-tenders who sneer at the potential of tidal power as an energy resource should perhaps be rammed into the mud of Cobscook Bay at low tide and asked what they think of the incoming, writhing wall of water.

It is easy, of course, for a contemplative naturalist to extol the beauties of the Eastport and Cobscook Bay waters; I who need not fight them for their clams and fish. The men and women who trade sea tales across the counter at Eastport's Wa-Co diner would be right to think me presumptuous, though they would use stronger words than that.

But the fact remains that theirs is a sea of beauty. And fury. And

Isabel Lewando

whispers. It grasps the soul and shakes it, destroying cobwebs and preconceptions.

* * *

When was the last time you sat in the woods without a stitch of clothing between your skin and the elements? I'm no evangelical nudist, but I must admit that as summer accelerates, my body itches to be unencumbered when I take to the woods. The temptation is sometimes too great to resist.

It's not easy, though, going naked in the woods. It is not "normal" and we must overcome not only a wealth of physical limitations, but a whole network of psychological hang-ups. There is a big difference between wearing skimpy clothing at the beach, where the footing is soft and the breezes soothing, and absolute nakedness in the woods. The smallest twig gouges into shoe-softened feet. Gently swaying branches become sadists' whips. The oddest parts of the body get sunburned and bug-bitten.

But it is an experience worth trying, if compromised by brevity and the retention of some sort of footwear.

The woodland animals are more trusting of the naked, perhaps reassured by the obvious absence of weapons and the knowledge that a naked 20th-century human is a pretty helpless creature. Birds become downright curious.

The greatest reward is largely intangible. It comes in the form of a sensation, an acceptance of both body and world as they are, not as we wish or imagine them to be. Huddled beneath the spready boughs of an evergreen during a sudden shower, the naked woods-wanderer begins to hear whispers. Primal sensations well from the soul and the ghosts of earlier wanderers flit among the trees. A hand stretches across the eons in welcome, a hand smaller and hairier than the one it stretches to grasp.

Things become elemental. A simple heap of small stones assumes great importance; not as a heap of stones, but as potential spear points, scrapers and cutting implements. Pick up a flat, palm-sized stone and strike its edges with another, heftier stone. The sound is an echo, a vibration rippling from the human womb.

Bodily functions become no more than that. Septic tanks and perfumed, brightly colored toilet paper seem laughable and alien. Squatting next to an appropriately broad-leafed maple, one merely adds to the deposits of the suddenly more kindred deer, raccoon and rabbit.

Food takes on a new dimension and value, its acquisition pivotal

Isabel Lewando

to survival rather than a convenient, albeit expensive, transaction. And what of meat? While only the long-term woodland visitor need answer the question, it does hover at the edge of the awakening mind. How does a naked, unarmed human slay and butcher a deer... or a rabbit? I once interviewed a young man who spent an entire year in the Pine Barrens of New Jersey — alone, naked and unarmed — and he suggested that all deer hunters should first do by hand what they wish to do with high-powered, scope-equipped firearms "so they'd really understand what they're doing."

We do, indeed, overburden ourselves with the trappings of civilization whenever we venture into the woods and nakedness is reserved for rare moments of utter solitude. We lose sight of who we

White-tailed Deer   Leonard Lee Rue III

really are, shrouding our beings in cloth and plastic and our minds in preconceptions.

Shared with another, nakedness becomes not nakedness, but humanness. Bodies become bodies, different in shape and color but reassuringly basic and beautifully functional. Even gender loses much of its significance in the uncompromising light of genuine nakedness.

We have come too far along the road of evolution to turn back. Constant nakedness has not been a human trait for eons, but it is a heritage that we cannot deny and which we should embrace on occasion, if only to remind us from whence we have come and how very much we have changed along the way.

Woodchuck / Groundhog / Groundchuck

GATHERING OF BEASTS

I don't know how my mother tolerated it, that steady carnival of beasts I brought home as a youngster. For a few years there, our playroom and cellar were genuine zoos of slithering, crawling, flying, jumping and swimming creatures. Nothing with fur, feathers, scales or shells escaped my grasp: frogs and toads, snakes, salamanders, turtles, birds, ants, caterpillers, squirrels and chipmunks . . . even a stray woodchuck or two.

Hardly a day passed when "The Beastboy" failed to catch his appointed animal. I shouldn't have.

It is with guilty sorrow that I now remember all too clearly the deaths of so many of my wild "pets." I recall saving a single baby garter snake by conducting a caesarian section on its dead mother, an operation of which I was then boastfully proud. But all the mother's young might well have survived if she had not been captured and caged in the first place, subjecting her to a lifestyle that was hardly conducive to the robust health necessary to bear and care for young.

There are babes in the woods and they should be left alone, as should their mothers, fathers, aunts, uncles, cousins and siblings.

Humans have a knack of taking pity on any animal that seems lost, hurt or otherwise unable to fend for itself. We put them in shoeboxes and take them home where we try to cram all sorts of noxious concoctions down their throats. More often than not, the hapless creatures soon become fertilizer for the rose garden.

The fact of the matter is that most animals have a far better shot at surviving if left to their own devices. Some tend to creep away for a time if ill or injured, lapsing into an energy-conserving lethargy until the malady has passed. They know what is best for them. We certainly do not.

One of our most common — and deadly — mistakes is to adopt a young animal on the erroneous premise that is has been abandoned. The most frequent victims of such good intentions are seals, raccoons, fawns and birds, most of whom have actually been purposefully left alone for a time by parents who must range far for food. Some, including fawns, are left alone for hours at a time by parents who know their distinctive scent can attract predators from considerable distances: the fawns themselves are virtually scentless.

Young birds sometimes leave their nests a bit early, driven out by flies, lice, belligerent siblings or a misplaced sense of adventure.

Black Bear Cub—2 months old Leonard Lee Rue III

White-tailed Deer Fawn   Irene Vandermolen

They should either be returned to their nests or left where they are: the parents of such prematurely homeless young generally continue to feed and, to what extent they can, protect them.

Many young animals, notably grouse and ducks, begin to travel with their parents shortly after birth, scattering into thickets or marshes at the approach of danger. It therefore should not be presumed that a lone youngster is indeed alone. Deer have been known to impassively watch as humans abscond with their young, but that is the exception and those animals which behave in an actively protective manner when their young are threatened represent yet another reason to leave the woodland young alone.

You can get hurt.

No one in his or her right mind would stand between a bear cub and its mother. Nor should the young of fishers and feral dogs, even of the tiny weasel, be interfered with. Their parents are more likely to attack an interloper than watch the proceedings, though most such attacks are threatening displays of ferocity and surprise, rather than actual attempts to injure or kill. A display can quickly turn into a very real and very injurious attack if the interloper does not heed the warning, however.

Eastern Chipmunk   Maine Fish & Game Dept.

The young themselves should not be underestimated in terms of self-preservation.

Young chipmunks and the like customarily regurgitate their most recent meal on whomever manages to catch them, but they can also bite, as can a variety of young animals. Others have an arsenal of talons, claws and beaks that can do surprising damage, particularly when aimed at the eyes of an attacker.

Diseases and parasitic infestations can be passed on from an animal parent to its young and hence on to anything or anyone who may come into contact with the young. Rabies, fleas, lice, worms, leeches and ticks are just a few of the afflictions that can be transmitted in such a fashion.

There are a few exceptions to the "hands-off" rule. Some injured young, such as birds with broken wings or fawns with seriously infected eyes — and the offspring of parents who have been killed — can reasonably be adopted, but their care should be entrusted to game farms, animal shelters and other such facilities. Unfortunately, most animal rescue organizations are already overtaxed by "adopted" animals.

Fortunately, it is now illegal to keep wild pets in the home. I wish that had been the case when I was an animal-grabbing youngster.

How many parents know that it is illegal to shoot migratory birds, with the exception of game birds in season? That includes almost every bird imaginable, from robins and warblers to starlings and cowbirds, and they need not be migrat*ing*, just migrat*ory*.

That is something to keep in mind when buying BB guns and slingshots for the children's birthday or Christmas presents. Many such weapons seem to wind up in the hands of youngsters who spend many an afternoon walking along country roads, shooting at anything that moves. For much of the spring and summer, each slain adult bird represents the deaths of several young.

* * *

Few animals can reasonably claim to have no enemies, but the skunk . . . well, it may not have many friends, but neither does it have many enemies to worry about.

One does not have to visit a woodlot, forest, field or park to meet a skunk because it is a creature of diverse habitat, ranging well into residential neighborhoods in search of garbage and the rodents and insects attracted to garbage. Perhaps because the skunk has no natural foes, it assumes that all the world is its do-

Striped Skunk Leonard Lee Rue III

main: it has yet to fully appreciate the hazards posed by cars, uninitiated dogs and irrational humans.

The skunk is a carnivorous mammal, specifically a member of the weasel family. Its distinctive anatomical feature is a pair of glands located at the base of its bushy tail. Each gland has a nipple-like opening surrounded by muscle. When contracted, the muscle forces a yellowish liquid from the glands with such strength and accuracy that a predator foolish enough to get within a dozen feet can usually expect to be hit between the eyes. On those rare occasions when the skunk misses its target, it simply fires again. It can fire as many as six times before its reserves are exhausted, but by that time its target is likely to be a mile or so away... and still running.

The liquid contained in the skunk's powerful glands is butyl mercaptan, an organic sulphur dioxide with an oil base that causes temporary blindness — as if the stench of the stuff is not enough. There are some debatable reports of persons being permanently blinded by the liquid, or musk.

Fortunately, the skunk almost always gives ample warning of its intentions. While it can fire in virtually any direction without aligning its body with its target, it normally turns its back on its target, stamps its feet, hisses and then — Look out! — raises its tail. Some delete the foot-stomping routine, but you can always count on some preparatory theatrics.

Despite its objectionable aspects, the skunk is a basically gentle creature that seldom uses its special defenses and actually seems to enjoy the company of humans. It can be easily (but illegally) domesticated and will endear itself to its keepers with its tidy nature and its taste for such household pests as rats, mice, moths, grasshoppers and beetles. It is customary and very wise to have the musk glands of house-bound skunks removed, although many have gone through a life of domestication without losing the weapons.

In addition to its most obvious "fault," the skunk is disliked because it has a definite taste for eggs and young birds. An improperly closed chicken coop is a skunk's paradise. Many a farmer has regretted the night he investigated what he assumed was a fox or weasel raid on his flock.

The skunk is primarily nocturnal, feeding from sunset to sunrise and spending the daylight hours in an underground den lined with leaves. It does not hibernate in the true sense of the term, but those living in the Northeast do sleep for several weeks when the winter going gets tough, awakening in February and March to mate. It is during the mating season and in the fall that a great many skunks perish on the highway. The spring fatalities are generally males, wandering far beyond their usual haunts in search of mates, while the fall casualties are most likely "kittens" recently weaned of parental care. Young skunks will, however, sometimes remain with a parent through their first winter.

It is during those seasons that we and our house pets are most likely to be fired upon, though it is reassuring to know that a skunk generally must be thoroughly provoked before it will use its weaponry. I have actually picked up a wild skunk that I mistook on a foggy night for a family cat and was not sprayed, but there is no telling what a young or sex-starved skunk will do, provoked or not.

Pets that have been sprayed should obviously be subjected to a thorough washing — outdoors. A good quantity of canned tomatoes or tomato paste rubbed into the pet's fur will help, but make certain that the animal is kept dry after the initial washing because the slightest dampness will only rejuvenate the remnants of spray still clinging to its fur.

Clothing that has been sprayed may never recover, but several successive washings in a heavy-duty cleanser might do the trick. Woe be to the person who is sprayed while garbed in an expensive evening gown or tuxedo!

Skunks do occasionally enter and take up residence in homes, but they very seldom will cause any problems unless provoked. Patience is the best tool for evicting a skunk: wait until it has departed for a night food foray and firmly cover its point of entry. Skunks which become barnyard or garden pests can be trapped in enclosed containers such as metal garbage cans and wooden barrels. Anchor the trap in an upright position, toss in a few sardines, broken eggs or catfood and lean a sturdy board against the trap, forming a ramp from the ground to the lip of the trap. Few skunks will spray inside a container from which they cannot escape — there always are exceptions — so those caught in such a trap can be transported with reasonable safety to a release site several miles away.

If the skunk is the stinker of the woodlot and field, the muskrat must be its protégé.

He isn't very pretty and his smell IS something to sneeze at, but the muskrat is one of the most engaging creatures one could hope to meet in a swampy back forty.

In a three-way beauty contest, even the most gorgeous muskrat

Muskrat   Leonard Lee Rue III

would have to stand in the wings while its neighbors waddled away with the top prizes; the beaver with the talent citation and the otter with the congeniality award. The three do share a few characteristics, however, not the least significant of which is a coat of fur of some commercial value. But the muskrat is definitely the poor cousin of the lot, the swamp's version of the reviled rat.

Musk-rat. The first syllable refers to the odor secreted by the animal's musk glands, an odor much weaker than but remindful of that produced by a skunk. The last syllable refers to its physical appearance: it does look like a rat and, in fact, is often mistaken for a giant "sewer" rat.

Thanks to the presence of two swampy ponds and a network of seasonal streams and sinkholes, our back forty is a haven for muskrats, a wet oasis in an otherwise fairly dry forest. It is both home and rest stop for the prolific animals, known to undertake 25-mile hikes to find uncrowded waters.

In the water, the muskrat is decidedly graceful, using its slightly flattened tail for steerage and webbed hind feet for locomotion. Because its tail is neither as large nor as flat as that of a beaver, it does not slap the foot-long appendage against the water to warn of approaching enemies; instead, it may launch its entire body from the water and, with a sharp squeak, dive for the safety of its stick-and-grass lodge or swamp-side burrow.

Underwater, it moves with considerable speed and ease, often trailing a stream of bubbles, and it can stay submerged for some 10 to 15 minutes.

On land, it is an apparently ungainly creature, its hunched body supported by stubby legs. But it is no slow-poke, traveling several miles in an evening with hardly a pause to catch its breath. Its gait may not be graceful, but it is functional. I once followed a muskrat from a woodland pond to a stream nearly a mile away, a trek that took no more than 45 minutes and led us through a pine grove and across a farmhouse lawn, driveway, state highway and brushy field. Of course, my presence several yards to the rear may have spurred the muskrat to unusual speeds, but I know the sight of a human escourting a bedraggled muskrat across a highway has the opposite effect on passing motorists.

Unlike the beaver, which can turn a small trickle of water into a full-fledged pond, the muskrat lacks the engineering capabilities to erect dams and therefore must search for suitably large and deep ponds, swamps, streams, backwaters and rivers in which to make its home. Depth is not terribly important, as a muskrat will stick it out in a shallow pond, such as the larger of our two that often utterly dries up in August and remains waterless for a month or two.

Escape options are important and the muskrat's first order of business upon finding a suitable home is the excavation of living quarters and tunnels in the banks bordering the water. It also is more than likely to erect one or more lodges in mid-water or hidden among the bushes and reeds. Its lodge is similar to that of the beaver, though constructed of less hefty materials and invariably smaller in size.

The bank burrows of the muskrat are its principal living quarters, access provided from beneath the water and leading to one or more chambers dug out of the soil above the water level, often beneath a tree's network of roots. Inside the chambers, a female muskrat will bear as many as five litters a year, each litter containing one to 10 young.

Needless to say, the muskrat is a reproductive machine nearly as proficient as the legendary rabbit, a fact that has had much to do with its ability to endure incredible trapping pressure and predation by a host of enemies, including coyotes, snakes, snapping turtles, large fish, owls, hawks, foxes, bobcats and, when winters are especially harsh and long, its own kind.

Thankfully, it has endured, showing an adaptability and tolerance equalled only by the white-tailed deer, woodchuck, coyote and a handful of other animals who must constantly vie with humans for space and food.

Among the animals consistently regarded as field and back-forty pests, perhaps the most widely despised and misunderstood is the groundchuck.

What? The "groundchuck"?

Yup, the groundchuck. I never did like the names "groundhog" and "woodchuck." The animal is not a pig, at least not in the swinely sense of the term, and it certainly does not hurl much wood. It does, however, chuck an awful lot of ground during its perilous lifetime.

By whatever name it is known, it has been shot, poisoned, gassed, zapped, trapped and dog-chased for centuries. Such treatment is often necessary in the interest of crop preservation but is, in many cases, excessive and ill-motivated, as well as accompanied by slurs on its character that are wholly unjustified. The fact of the matter is that the groundchuck has its good points, though not quite enough to outweigh the bad behavior it

Woodchuck / Groundhog / Groundchuck Irene Vandermolen

exhibits in the neighborhood of vegetable gardens, flower beds and young orchards.

If, for example, the earthworm is so universally admired as an aerator and fertilizer of the soil, what of the groundchuck? A single groundchuck moves, aerates and otherwise improves the quality of 100 to an astonishing 700-plus pounds of soil during the excavation of its burrow. And when it dies, the groundchuck's own remains perform one final act of fertilization in a subterranean fashion that just is not true of surface-dwelling creatures.

Earthworms, of course, do not attack peas, carrots, radishes, beans, melons, flowers, cucumbers and . . . But it is time we accepted the fact that without the persecuted 'chuck our soil would be less capable of supporting such bumper crops of these and other delights.

An additional point in the groundchuck's favor is the service its burrow performs for a variety of other animals. Rabbits, foxes, skunks and others use handy 'chuck burrows to hibernate, leaving the excavator undisturbed in a hibernation chamber which it seals off from the rest of the maze. That is one reason a groundchuck burrow should not be gassed between October and April: the intended victim will not be the only animal to perish. If gassing is the only solution to a particularly nettlesome groundchuck problem, the deed should be done in May or early June when both adults and young are home, alone.

Killing groundchucks actively engaged in garden raids is one thing, but the fairly common "sport" of hunting 'chucks who reside miles from the nearest pea trellis makes no sense at all. If indeed they are pests and "varmints" because they raid our gardens, exactly what are the humans who venture miles from hearth and home to raid groundchuck burrows?

In the late 1950s, five jet-black 'chucks were found in two Maine towns and despite the rarity of their color, worthlessness of their fur and their considerable distance from active gardens, they were quickly shot and displayed for eager newspaper photographers. The man who found and shot them proudly exclaimed that he had meted out similar fates to an average of 100 'chucks each year for several years.

Except for its proven taste for vegetables and, on rare occasions, the bark of young fruit trees, the groundchuck is an intriguing and basically harmless creature whose domestic habits could be a model for many a human household.

Excavated with powerful forefeet and teeth, the 'chuck's 10- to 40-foot burrow represents a zenith in animal efficiency, sporting at least one central bedroom and several secondary chambers, including some reserved specifically as bathrooms. Because very little food is brought directly into the burrow, the only worrisome source of filth is the animal's own waste, but it takes care of that by plugging up any bathroom that becomes dangerously overloaded.

The burrow itself is generally dug on a well-drained hillside and while the 'chuck prefers the protection of thickets, it will set up housekeeping in open fields and woodlands if the dietary factors are right. A groundchuck utopia would be a dry, rocky hillside cloaked with brambles, blueberry and dogwood and located about 50 yards from an unfenced garden patch.

Most burrows have more than one entrance and some have as many as four or five. Abandoned burrows are relished as home and haven by a veritable zoo of other animals and should not be plugged unless they pose hazards to hikers and horseback riders.

Much as I enjoy groundchucks, I am not foolish enough to contend they should never be gassed or gunned. Their numbers have so drastically increased with the transformation of forest into farmland that they, like the white-tailed deer, have indeed become pests in many localities. But not all groundchucks are pests, just as not all people are bad because some happen to be murderers. Those whose burrows are situated more than 300 or so yards from gardens probably do not pose much of a threat to anyone's pantry, though their offspring might and therefore should be watched when they begin to seek out spots to dig their own burrows.

Animals, like people, should be presumed to be "innocent until proven guilty."

* * *

Ever since Adam and Eve ate of that bitterest of fruit, the snake has been the uncontested symbol of human moral decay, a creature vilified and feared.

In the rocky mesquite country of the West and the deep swamps of the South, that fear is partially justified, but the snake's vilification is entirely unearned. It is an animal — a reptile, to be precise — that merits our attention and, to a large degree, our affection and gratitude.

The back forty's snakes are utterly harmless, as are those found throughout most of the Northeast. They are as afraid of humans as humans generally are of them and will quickly and quietly disappear at the first hint of human intrusion. Only when surprised,

Eastern Garter Snake Leonard Lee Rue III

harrassed or otherwise threatened will a snake strike, exercising a defense mechanism that is hardly unique to its kind.

Only once in the score-plus years that I have been poking into rock piles and other reptilian haunts have I been "snake-bit," and I deserved it. A snakebite is not something to fear, unless the snake is poisonous. A snake's fangs are exceptionally clean and scalpel-sharp and the resultant wound is seldom painful. A bee sting is far worse ... and far more likely in both city and snake country.

Snakes are enthralling creatures, possessing several hundred backbones, deaf in the human sense of the term, able to remove their entire skins without a crease or wrinkle and, in some cases, capable of going without food for more than a year. They are found everywhere on earth, save some isolated islands and in the colder regions toward both poles.

The most common of the Northeast's snakes is the garter, whose favorite haunts are somewhat rocky, overgrown fields, although they can be found most anywhere. The garter snake reaches a maximum length of some 20 inches, about twice the size of the almost equally common but effectively camouflaged and therefore less frequently observed grass or green snake. There are a number of water snakes in the region, inhabiting the edges of ponds, lakes, swamps and bogs. Perhaps the most attractive of our native snakes is the ring-necked, a small and secretive fellow with a yellow-orange band about its neck.

Two poisonous snakes, the "rattler" and the copperhead, once were counted among the region's snake population, but our age-old fears, manifested by organized snake hunts and impulsive clubbings, have banished them from virtually all of New England. Now and then, there are reports of a rattlesnake den being discovered, but such reports usually bear the footnote that the finder "exterminated" the inhabitants.

It is the manner in which snakes eat which seems most repulsive to the human mind and eye. Because snakes lack chewing teeth, they must swallow their prey whole and they are perfectly suited to the task. Those teeth which snakes do have are curved backward to ease the swallowing process and the muscles which provide its means of locomotion are quickly adapted as swallowing implements. Indeed, the snake seems more to move slowly over its meal than to swallow it.

Getting something whose girth is greater than its own into a snake's mouth may seem an impossible proposition, but the snake again is equipped with all the necessary tools. It simply detaches its lower jaw, making its mouth — indeed, its entire head — as flexible as its body and enabling it to cope with a meal double or even triple its own body width.

People seem also to find the snake's practice of shedding or molting its skin rather unsavory, despite the fact that humans are forever doing the same thing, though in a less dramatic and more "genteel" manner. Pressing its body into a narrow crevice, a snake will rub off its drying and tightening skin several times a year. It is not unusual to find dozens of complete skins littering the ground about especially suitable crevices, complete even to the thin skin which covers all snakes' eyes, allowing them to go through life without benefit of eyelids. An unbroken skin looks rather like an opaque and very brittle sock.

Snakes do not "hear" as humans do. They rely not on airborne sounds, but on vibrations in the ground to pinpoint prey and predator alike. Their mechanisms of smell are similarly unusual. Snakes are equipped with traditional nostrils and many of the associated tools of the smelling trade, but they also have two cavities — chemoreceptors — in their mouths which give them an added dimension of smell. Using their ever-moving tongues, snakes place miniscule particles from the ground into these cavities, where they are analyzed for any evidence of a friend or foe who may have passed the same way.

Despite their unusual and, to many eyes, distasteful practices, snakes are almost entirely beneficial creatures. They have been known to rob chicken coops of both young birds and eggs, but such depradations are more than countered by the volume of gluttonous and disease-carrying rodents they devour. It has been estimated that some snakes, particularly the larger varieties which frequent Midwestern fields and barns, eat as many as 150 mice during the six months when they are constantly active.

A number of misconceptions and myths are associated with snakes, as though we require tangible evidence of their diabolical character. It is ridiculous to suppose, for example, that snakes hypnotize their prey: many animals, including the natural prey of snakes, defend themselves by remaining motionless at the approach of danger, but they are by no means hypnotized. Neither is it true that snakes can grasp their tails in their mouths and roll down hills, or that they swallow their young, or that they are slimey, or that they are related to worms . . . .

* * *

I cannot remember when I met my first butterfly, but I don't suppose anyone does. They simply flutter into one's life, ethereal visitors from fairy tales and dreams.

Both butterflies and moths are members of the lepidoptera order of insects, as are the curious skippers which can best be described as something of a cross between their two cousins. In the vast insect kingdom, only the order of beetles has more members than the lepidoptera, whose representatives can be found on every continent except Antarctica.

We are more acquainted with the butterflies than with the moths, simply because the latter are predominantly nocturnal and seldom sufficiently large or colorful to demand attention. A brightly colored and intricately patterned butterfly, adrift against a blue summer sky, is far more eye-catching than a small, dull-colored moth flattened almost invisibly against the equally dull bark of a tree.

There are exceptions to the dull moth-brilliant butterfly "rule," of course: the luna moth is vibrant green in color with long wing "tails" and the superficially unexciting hawk moths display a rainbow of pink, brown and black when their wings are fully exposed.

Butterflies and moths are more specifically different in physical terms. Moths have fatter, stubbier bodies than butterflies and are hairier in appearance. Furthermore, the antennae of moths are usually branched and fern-like while those of the butterfly tend to be lengthier, smoother and flattened or lobed at the tips.

As one might expect, the physical differences between the two reflect differences in their behavior. The fern-like antennae of the

Monarch Butterfly   Isabel Lewando

night-flying moths, for example, enable them to more easily detect food by smell. The day-flying butterflies, on the other hand, are more visually adept and their antennae are of correspondingly lesser importance, though nonetheless critical to their survival.

These "rules" of differentiation are hardly firm. There are many moths whose antennae are decidedly butterfly-like. There are also moths with smooth bodies and butterflies with slightly hairy bodies. And some butterflies are as dull or ever duller in color than the typically drab moth.

Moths and their larvae, particularly the latter, are generally more destructive than butterflies and their larvae, as anyone who has dealt with tent caterpillars, gypsy moths or clothes moths is well aware. But neither the moths nor the butterflies transmit plant diseases, as do a myriad of other insects. Their larvae merely chew their way to infamy, variously decimating evergreens, fruit and ornamental trees, vegetables and flowers.

On the other hand, butterflies and moths assist in the pollination of countless flowering plants, though they are not as proficient as the bee, and it can be argued that they assure the maturity and reproductive powers of more plants than their larvae destroy.

The most distinctive features of moths and butterflies are their wings. All but a very few species have two pairs, one pair positioned on each side of the thorax, the middle of three body segments diagnostic of all insects. The wings come in all shapes, sizes and colors and some, especially among the moths, bear distinctly eye-like markings that allow them to be mistaken for owls or other large creatures by their innumerable enemies.

The proboscis of a moth or butterfly is also distinctive. Consisting of a single sucking tube, nerves, muscles and a pair of tracheal passages, the proboscis is the mouth of the butterfly or moth. There is some evidence that it may, in fact, be the evolutionary extension — literally and otherwise — of a jaw structure not radically different from that of its present-day, chewing larvae. The lepidopterae do not taste their food as we do, unless you happen to have tongues on your knees. Alighting on a flower, a moth or butterfly "tastes" the presence of sweet nectar or other plant juices with its legs, triggering the proboscis to unwind from beneath its head and to plunge into the flower. Again, the "rule" is not universal: many have "taste buds" of a sort located on short stalks at the base of the proboscis.

It is safe to say that the moths and butterflies are among the world's most varied inhabitants. We know them primarily as colorful additions to a summer afternoon or as nettlesome closet or crabapple pests, but there is more to them than meets the eye.

* * *

It looked like a three-inch strip of thick, dark-brown leather glued to the outside of his right foot. Except that it moved.

Matt knew what it was and he didn't like it one bit.

With a wild-eyed yell and a sweep of a desperate hand, he hurled the leathery creature to the sand where it curled into a gritty ball. Judy and I coaxed him back to the water of the rushing stream and rinsed the grit from his foot, revealing another eight wedged between his toes, each no more than a half-inch in length.

Bloodsucker.

The title is deserved but hardly tells the whole tale. "Leech" is the term I prefer, a title that separates the creature from the yoke of an exaggerated — or at least over-emphasized — habit. I do not like leeches any more than the next person. Like Matt, I abhor the thought of them "planted" on my skin. But I am older and have met enough of them to at least separate unreasonable fear from plain loathing.

I have even come to consider the leech a rather lovely creature, when it is on the move in open water. It undulates gracefully through the liquid, an echo and a user of the gentle currents and tiers of temperature and light. It is the water's version of the vulture, soaring with alert ease from one rocky aerie to another, searching all the while for food.

Leeches are members of the Hirudinea class of segmented worms, of which there are more than 300 species inhabiting most parts of the world. Measuring up to eight inches in length, all have 34 distinct segments, one or more pairs of light-sensitive cells or "eyes" and disk-like suckers at each end of their bodies, their mouths located at the center of the smaller sucker at their slimmer ends. Sexually, they are monoecious, carrying both male and female reproductive organs, although they are incapable of self-fertilization.

Not all leeches are bloodsuckers. Some feed on decaying vegetable or animal matter. Nor do all live in water. In the more tropical regions, several species lead arboreal lives, waiting patiently on a moist leaf or fern for an animal to pass. Others prefer the darkness of the soil or sand. A few can be found at sea.

Those which plague humans are members of the Gnathobdellidae family and are temporarily parasitic in behavior, attaching themselves to hosts long enough to dine. Most have tiny, three-toothed jaws that puncture the skin to initiate a flow of blood, a flow that is maintained by the secretion of an anticoagulant called hirudin into the wound. The hirudin (from which the class of worms gets its name) also often causes the wound to bleed long after the leech has had its fill and dropped off.

Until this century, physicians commonly used certain leeches for "bloodletting," releasing presumably "bad" blood from wounds and bruises or for the treatment of more general maladies. A headache, for example, was treated by attaching a leech to each temple.

In very general terms, the leeches which swimmers and waders in the Northeast must contend with inhabit freshwater ponds, lakes, swamps and streams. They dislike cold, fast water but cannot be ruled out of any situation: I once had a leech attach itself to my armpit while I sat in a bone-chilling, bone-jarring waterfall above timberline. Those that do inhabit fast-moving streams, including those which selected Matt as their host, are seldom seen, except on the skin, but can be found beneath rocks, logs and other havens, secured by their strong suckers.

Once a leech has become firmly attached, it can be difficult to remove without the proper equipment. The hot head of a wooden match will do the trick (just as it is a sure-fire method of convincing a tick to withdraw its head from beneath the skin), as will dry sand or ashes sprinkled liberally over the leech's wet body. My favorite method is to dust the creature with a hefty dose of table salt. Anything that prevents it from staying cool and moist will work.

Anyone who swims in water where leeches are likely to be found should examine themselves upon leaving the water, keeping in mind the fact that because they need to stay moist and avoid direct light, they are most likely to attach themselves to the skin of the armpits, between the toes and fingers, behind the ears and within body cavities.

The presence of a leech on one's skin isn't cause for the panic that normally accompanies such a discovery. It is not going to cause any great pain or discomfort and it neither withdraws an excessive amount of blood nor injects any poisons. I would venture that the average outdoors person loses more blood in a day to mosquitoes during their peak season than any single leech could possibly extract.

You might even take the time to watch it at work for a minute or two.

Isabel Lewando

SKULKING, HAYING & SUCH

It is the skulking season on the back forty.

"Skulking" is the fine art of sneaking hither and yon, and this is the season in which the art must be practiced to perfection if one wishes to keep in touch with the goings-on in woodlot, field and backyard.

It is the season of the young, the time for the birds and beasts to prepare their young for adulthood. The first broods of starlings have already been fledged from their nests tucked away in holes beneath the barn roof and the single phoebe's nest perched on a beam inside the barn will bid adieu to its four occupants within the week.

The fattest of the two woodchucks — er, groundchucks — whose burrow includes the barn's entire subterranean drainage network lost a considerable amount of weight a couple of weeks ago and I suspect there are two or three 'chuck pups hidden away within the excavated and borrowed maze.

Whether furred or feathered, the new parents and parents-to-be have fallen silent. The din of song and chase that filled the days of May has faded to a gentle and sporadic echo. The creatures are going about their business of parenting, a business that demands alertness and silence. Even the usually boisterous blue jays and the loudly argumentative raccoons are mute or nearly so.

It is with good reason they have fallen silent. A nest or burrow is a fixed object and while its newborn occupants are not exactly stationary, they may as well be where the fox, weasel, cat, snake and owl are concerned. Once discovered by a predator, a nest or den is a virtually defenseless target, its occupants as table-ready — and often as brittle — to the hungry hunter as a bag of potato chips is to you or me.

Parental stealth and silence increase the odds of survival by decreasing the odds of detection. No nest or den is truly secure, however, just as no human habitation is entirely safe from the ravages of the tornado or hurricane.

The construction and configuration of an animal's home provide its first line of defense. Birds' nests are carefully situated so as to be hidden or inaccessible to likely predators: the warbler's nest deep within a bramble thicket is hidden and that of the oriole dangling 60 feet above the ground is inaccessible. Those nests which are readily accessible, such as that of the whippoorwill, are camouflaged, as are the eggs and/or the parents who tend them.

Eastern Bluebird   Leonard Lee Rue III

The beaver protects itself and its young by erecting a sturdy stick lodge some distance from the shore of its pond, the lodge entrances hidden beneath the surface of the water. The raccoon's den is high in a hollow tree or deep within a rock pile that is easily defended against small predators and inaccessible to their larger foes.

All that planning and labor would be of little use unaccompanied by stealth and silence. Many birds refuse to go directly to their nests for fear an oft-repeated route will soon be detected. A bobolink will drop into the tall grass several yards from its nest and "walk" the rest of the way to its doorstep. Warblers often approach their nests in a cautiously round-about fashion, flitting from bush to bush until assured they are alone or their actions have been interpreted as those of a feeding rather than a homeward-bound bird.

When their young are threatened, many birds and some other animals will try their best to distract the invader by feigning an injury designed to convince the predator that it is far easier prey than its young. Few forget to warn their neighbors, however, breaking the silence with a chorus of cries which the well-informed birdwatcher can easily distinguish from the other, more routine sounds of summer.

As the animals have become stealthy and silent, so must the devout animal-watcher. My back forty excursions nowadays take on rather bizarre overtones as I try my utmost to be unobstrusive . . . if a 175-pound, binocular- and camera-laden human truly can be unobtrusive.

Sneaking up on the ducks in the larger of the two ponds is a time-consuming proposition as I press my body, reeking of insect repellent, against the ground. Holding camera and binoculars before as a soldier holds his carbine, I worm and wiggle my way to a blind at the edge of the pond. More often than not, the ducks either are absent or have detected my approach and are doing their own skulking among the tangled bayberry bushes on the opposite side.

It then becomes a question of waiting — perhaps for hours — or moving on to other subjects, flowers and rocks being the most enticing because they cannot run, crawl or fly away. But it is the woodlot's mobile inhabitants who are too enticing to resist, whether for "shooting" with camera or observing, undetected and at close quarters.

So the stealthy quest resumes. Stealth against stealth. Skulking against skulking. Success is elusive: a human trying to match

Maine Development Commission

stealth with a duck is rather like a turtle racing a rabbit. But there is ever the hope that today will be the day.

* * *

They are haying this weekend at the farm in New Hampshire, plotting the process like military strategists.

The boys and their grandpa stand in the midst of the undulating lines of drying hay, watching the tractors clatter back and forth, followed by the stake-sided trucks and the heavers of bales. Even Tiana, the doctorate-holding cousin who need not concern herself with such matters, is muscling the heavy bales onto the trucks.

It is one of those perfect weekends in the Contoocook River Valley. The peaks and ridges of Monadnock and Crotched Mountains are firmly etched against a blue, cloudless sky while the steeple of the Unitarian church in the center of the village below is similarly etched against the green of the hills beyond. Wrens bubble from the lilac and smokebush as swallows dip and wheel overhead.

Watching the boys and their grandpa and feeling the essence of the day, I recall days 20-odd years ago when another young boy and his grandpa trudged the farm roads and fields and paths. My grandpa loved the farm and his eyes would sparkle and gleam as we discovered and talked of jack-in-the-pulpits, poison ivy, tree swallows and red-backed salamanders. I think I knew, as did he, that time was then weaving one of its eternal circles.

Grandpa soon would no longer be able to make the trip from Cambridge and the "Yellow House" would pass to his three daughters. One, my mother, had been born in the southeast bedroom and all had spent their growing-up summers here, weaving their own circles and memories.

And now their children have grown up, weaving similar tapestries and bringing their children to taste the elixir that is "the farm." Summoning them from California, Connecticut, Vermont and Maine, the farm is calling its children home to renew old ties, to add a few more threads to another arc of the circle. They bring new spouses, new children and new visions, but the memories and the constants are there, as if hewn into the trunk of the great oak on the front lawn.

Grandpa used to wheel me from barn to house and back again in an ancient wheelbarrow that still can do a good day's work. On this haying day nearly three decades later, my sons are wheeled by their grandpa from barn to house and back again. Giggles echo

Guy Gannett Publishing Co.

across the years. My mother smiles, remembering... perhaps aching just a bit.

The smell of fresh-mown hay does not change, nor does the redness of the apples at picking-time. The flat-topped rock that has served as table to countless picnics will always be there, though the pines about it may one day yield to other trees and the rhododendron that Judy and I planted in its shadow to celebrate our honeymoon may vanish.

And the memories will always be there. Long after my sons have wheeled their grandchildren from barn to house and back again in the ancient wheelbarrow, they will linger in the grass and the trees.

I wonder: do memories have memories?

We used to hear them into midsummer, their unmistakable calls ringing across the night-draped orchards and hayfields above the Contoocook River.

WHIP-poor-*WILL*... WHIP-poor-*WILL*... WHIP-poor-*WILL*....

My sister Sara, I remember, was a little frightened by the din, though I think my malicious evening readings from Edgar Allen Poe had a hand in that.

It has been years since the whippoorwills sang at the farm, thanks to a changing environment and the blossom-time use of pesticides dispersed over the orchards by low-flying helicopters or groaning tank trucks. I cannot remember exactly when the orchards and fields fell silent, but there was indeed a "silent spring" at the farm.

We do hear the whippoorwills now and then on our back forty, but only briefly as they pause on their journeys to more placid quarters to the north. Isolated as it may be from the hubbub of city or town, the back forty is still too tightly ringed by roads and too consistently punctured by hikers and dogs to suit the birds.

Like the loon, the whippoorwill is a bird of solitude, preferring mature or nearly mature hardwood forests to the manicured or cut-over woodlots of suburbia. It is even becoming scarce in relatively tranquil rural areas where the public thirst for firewood and recreation is having a profound impact on all wildlife.

The whippoorwill is a fascinating bird little-known to all but the most ardent of birdwatchers.

It is a member of the nightjar or goatsucker family, the latter designation reflecting the once common belief that it uses its cavernous mouth to drain milk from the teats of livestock. The mouth of the 10-inch bird is, in fact, used to scoop night-flying insects

Whippoorwill in threatening posture Leonard Lee Rue III

from the air. Strictly nocturnal — unlike its close relative, the nighthawk — the whippoorwill flies on near-silent wings, mouth agape with long bristles at each corner to facilitate the trapping of insects.

During the daylight hours, the weak-footed, brownish bird sits without moving on the forest floor or perches lengthwise — never crosswise — on a log or branch. Its coloration so closely matches the browns of its customary habitat that it is very rarely seen by the woods wanderer and only slightly more often detected by predators.

The whippoorwill's calling begins at dusk, just as the thrushes are falling silent and the peepers are warming up. A single bird may utter its namesake call a hundred times or more without pause, and many of its pauses are so brief as to barely qualify as such. The calling, which serves to attract mates and inform others of territorial claims, usually ends around midnight, but it may continue until dawn on especially moonlit nights when the bird is likely to spend less time on the wing. It is the clearest of the night's many voices, the aria of an opera resplendent with the music of frogs, insects, bats and owls. It is also a reminder that the night holds much about which we know very little.

Alas, the call is seldom heard today where once it was as routine as the buzz of mosquitoes.

They were as the grasses on the prairie, legion in number and seemingly secure from all but the fickle weather. Their migrating flocks sometimes passed unceasingly for days, blotting out the sun, and their nesting colonies often blanketed a thousand acres or more.

They were the passenger pigeons, beautiful and gentle birds. Until the arrival on this continent of the Europeans, they were indeed secure, but because they were also tasty they were doomed.

A single blast from a shotgun or scattergun could bring down dozens of the birds, but the most effective and the cheapest method of "collecting," as it was called, was the nighttime raid on nesting and roosting colonies. They were often gassed with burning sulphur, but more frequently were blinded by bright lights, knocked from their perches and pummeled to death.

The last of the passenger pigeons died in a Cincinnati zoo in 1914, a victim and a symbol of human greed and stupidity. It is hardly alone in the pantheon of animals and plants whose disappearances were caused by similar, human acts.

The Labrador duck, great auk, Carolina parakeet and heath hen were all good table fare and consequently are no longer with us. The similarly tasty Eskimo curlew, which had the suicidal habit of staying with wounded or slain members of its vast flocks, has probably also vanished.

Among those animals endangered or severely displaced by the onslaught of civilization are the bison, wild turkey, whooping crane, green sea turtle, peninsular pronghorn antelope, American crocodile, Utah prairie dog....

The North American "endangered" list surpasses 200, but it is safe to say that virtually all animals have declined in numbers or range since the settlement of Jamestown. There are several exceptions: the rock dove or common pigeon, white-tailed deer, gray squirrel, wood rat and others. But they *are* exceptions.

The term "endangered" — meaning an animal or plant that is

threatened by extinction — is significantly over-used by federal bureaucrats and environmentalists; not because it is inaccurate, but because it reflects the tendency to address the problem only when it is too late — or too costly — to provide a remedy.

The Eskimo curlew might be thriving today had we learned anything from the demise of the passenger pigeon.

The federal government has spent millions of dollars to learn if the black-footed ferret is still alive in the South Dakota foothills. A couple of decades ago, it would have cost perhaps one-tenth as much to avoid the question altogether by acquiring and closing the animal's last known breeding area.

Everywhere we look, there are animals that may face the ferret's fate in a matter of decades.

The wolf has disappeared from an estimated 99 percent of its former range. There are less than 130 whooping cranes left in the wild and each is carefully monitored and tracked — at great expense — by government zoologists. At last count, there were less than a dozen breeding female American crocodiles.

The cry of the ivory-billed woodpecker is still heard now and then in the deep forests of Louisiana, but none have been seen for years. The Kirtland's warbler nests in three or four Michigan counties in ever-dwindling numbers. The California condor is alive but almost certainly doomed. The Eastern cougar may still cling to a few isolated wilderness tracts in Canada and perhaps in northernmost Maine.

We are the culprits. The Tecopa pupfish, insignificant by our worldly standards, vanished when its unique habitat was compromised by the combining and rechanneling of a few California springs to supply a bathhouse. Vacation condominiums and luxury "retreats" have pushed the peregrine falcon to the limits of its ability to survive.

The question of how much we should do and spend — if anything — to avert extinction among the other animals is clouded by another question. Might not some be destined for extinction anyway, no matter what we have done or may choose to do?

The answer to the latter query is certainly "yes," otherwise we would be sharing the land with dinosaurs, mastodons and an array of beasts whose disappearance had nothing to do with human behavior.

Questions, however, have the knack of raising more questions.

What of the human race . . . . ?

* * *

Among the countless miracles of the back forty and backyard, metamorphosis is perhaps the most mysterious, no matter how concisely it may be explained in blandly biological terms.

While the process itself is sufficiently mysterious, it becomes downright awesome when contemplated in relation to the human life experience. Does it hold some clues to the conquest of such human maladies as cancer, birth defects and organ degeneration? What can it tell us of our own prenatal development?

Very simply stated, metamorphosis — a term adopted from the Greek word for "transform" — is the process by which some invertebrates change from one form to another. Complete metamorphosis is a four-stage affair, typified by the egg-caterpiller-pupa-adult cycle of the butterfly. The superficial facts of the cycle are plain enough, but almost unfathomable complexity befogs contemplation of its various phases.

Using the butterfly as an example, a typically metamorphic creature is "born" from an egg and contains a juvenile hormone called neotenin, secreted by a gland called the corpus allatum. Secretion of the hormone continues through the larval or caterpiller stage and in a matter of days or weeks is cut off by such atmospheric changes as the shortening of daylight hours.

The halt of the neotenin secretion "tells" the larva to seek out a dry, protected place in which to enter the pupal stage of the cycle. Grasping an appropriate projection or surface, the larva sheds its skin for a final time — having done so throughout its larval stage in order to accommodate a rapidly expanding body — to reveal a chrysalis or cocoon, a generally brownish cylinder- or mummy-like object which among the moths is often covered with fine "hair."

It is during the pupal stage, which may last only days or continue through the winter, that the most astonishing of the process's many mysteries occurs. The insect's tissues break down and its organs vanish. It is reduced to a formless mass of liquid.

But the shell of the pupa whispers of what is to come, its surface faintly indented or otherwise marked with the curves and lines of wings, eyes, thorax, abdomen and antennae. It seems a mold, a blueprint for the now liquid creature's final transformation.

Choreographed by hormones, the liquid gradually coagulates and reforms. New organs and tissues are created. The chrysalis may become opaque or clear, revealing the colors of the "new" creature within. The shell then splits and the butterfly emerges to hang for a time in the sunlight, drying and unfolding its wings.

The "how" of the process is easier to explain than the "why," although it seems that the lengthy pre-adulthood of metamorphic creatures assures a minimum of juvenile-parent food competition. Caterpillers, for instance, normally dine on leaves and grasses while their jawless parents are nectar "drinkers." The strict food limitations of larvae and adults are so vastly different that only metamorphosis can see to it that the physical changes necessary to attain adulthood do occur properly.

Collecting caterpillers for the purpose of observing the metamorphic process is an ancient hobby, one far less domestically disruptive than most collecting hobbies of youngsters and adults. There are, however, some guidelines to follow if the process is to be properly carried out.

Caterpillers are very choosy eaters and therefore should not be collected unless their natural food can be readily identified and also collected. A plant on which a caterpiller is found is almost invariably that on which it dines.

Tent Caterpillars   Anita Finn

Monarch Butterfly   Guy Gannett Publishing Co.

Place the caterpiller in a well-ventilated, dry container — a large jar with screening over its mouth will do — and add a few leaves of its favorite fare, cleaning the jar and replacing the leaves at least once each day. A rock, twig or piece of cardboard can be added to provide necessary shade and to act as an anchor for the forthcoming pupa.

Do not place the container in direct sunlight: overheating is as dangerous to the soft-bodied caterpiller as it is to a human. The conditions within the container should essentially echo those of the caterpiller's natural habitat in terms of illumination, temperature, humidity and vegetation. If your specimen is of the wintering-over variety, place the container in an unheated location when the weather turns cool so that its occupant will be subjected to the conditions required for the completion of its metamorphic cycle.

Then, sit back and ponder what Shelley called the "ante-natal tomb where butterflies dream of the life to come."

Young Raccoons   Leonard Lee Rue III

MOVING ON

Last month it was the "skulking season" on the back forty; now it is "moving day."

The young birds and beasts whose parents were so protectively silent a few short weeks ago are now on the move, testing wings and legs that must work perfectly if they are to complete the perilous journey from infancy to adulthood.

While weeding the corn patch a couple of steamy afternoons ago, I was distracted by a chorus of yowls and squeaks coming from the ditch that parallels the roadway and into which babbles the small stream which seeps from the flanks of the woodlot. Huddled beneath a slab of concrete covering a culvert were four young raccoons, bedraggled packages of noise that seemed all eyes and noses.

More curious than afraid, they took turns thrusting their heads into the sunlight to stare briefly at the two-legged creature looming above them, squeaking occasionally to one another as if relaying some new data on the intruder. Now and then, one would tumble backward into the darkness of the culvert, belly- or back-flopping into the murky water.

Like many of the young seals found along the New England coast at this time of the year, the raccoons were neither lost nor abandoned. Their mother was close-by, waiting impatiently on the opposite side of the road, urging her offspring on with subdued yaps and growls. After one more glance at the comedic troupe, I returned to the corn patch, wondering if their mother had made note of its location in order to return just when the ears are "in milk." Probably: raccoons are uncanny when it comes to judging the maturity of corn.

Elsewhere within the back forty, other young are on the move.

Cloaked from beak to tail in thick down, a young wood duck plummets from a hole in a dead pine to the water of the larger pond some 30 feet below. A second chick appears at the mouth of the nest, hesitates and jumps. A third ... A fourth ... Bobbing like frayed corks, they vanish into the thick shrubbery and weeds with their mother. They are late hatching and I worry that they will not be airborne by the time the pond is locked again in ice.

Here and there among the pin cherries bordering the lawn, young catbirds, robins and starlings grasp wind-bounced limbs, squawking incessantly for their food-bearing parents. No human could be as exhaustively attentive to his or her offspring as are these parents.

Young Crested Flycatcher Leonard Lee Rue III

A young chipmunk meanders onto the driveway and twitches as the hot surface of the blacktop stabs its feet. It scuttles into the shade beneath the pickup truck, snuggles up against a cool tire for a few minutes and then plunges into the grass bordering the busy roadway. Like a cutting horse, I move between it and the roadway, gently redirecting the ignorant youth toward the woods behind the farmhouse.

The retreating waters of the two ponds, too, are swarming with young.

Half-inch tadpoles wander with apparent aimlessness through the brown liquid or cling to strands of submerged vegetation, their circular mouths sucking up tiny organic particles. Very few will live long enough to leave the water as frogs and toads: the dragonfly nymphs are abroad, drawing the meaty tadpoles to them with long, pincher-tipped tongues.

The mortality rate among the back forty young is high. Even if the wood duck young had hatched on schedule, three to five weeks ago, perhaps half could expect to leave the ponds. At least one of the raccoons will fall victim to fox, automobile or disease. The natural deaths from disease and predation are not distressing, but there are distressing deaths among the young at this time of year.

Domestic cats and dogs wreak havoc among the woodland young and their parents, but it requires human indifference to set the deadly process in motion. More distressing still is the direct interference of humans, the kind that cannot be dismissed on the grounds of ignorance, just as the commission of a crime cannot be excused because the criminal was ignorant of the law.

How many broods of birds are lost because their parents are felled by BB guns or slingshots? How many mice, snakes and chipmunks are flattened beneath the tires of trail bikes? How many loons and ducks are harrassed to death by boaters? How many "abandoned" squirrels, raccoons and woodchucks die in kitchens and livingrooms while their parents pace frantically outside? How many tadpoles suffocate in aquariums?

Too many. Far too many.

Its eyes still closed and its beak still tipped with shreds of an "egg tooth," the baby sparrow hawk lay curled into a tiny ball beneath the barn eaves.

It peeped frantically as I cradled it gently in my hands, examining its frail body for signs of broken bones and wounds. Despite the fall from its nest some 40 feet above, the bird seemed unin-

Sparrow Hawk Nestling   Leonard Lee Rue III

jured. It was nonetheless near death from starvation and exposure to the hot sun.

Matt was summoned from his chair in front of the television and unlocked the barn as I kept the bird cupped in my hands. It had struggled weakly at first but slowly relaxed in the warm shadows of my palms and fingers.

Sparrow hawks have nested in the barn eaves for years, gaining access through a hole cut in the underside board for unknown reasons by an unknown former owner. The nest area itself is about two feet long and a foot deep and was open to the interior of the barn before I boarded it up several years ago to protect the niche from our roving cats.

Matt pried the board loose. A trio of wide-eyed, healthy nestlings were crammed into a far corner, staring intently at the intruders. It hardly seemed possible that the weakling in my hands belonged to the same family and I pondered the dangers it would face upon being returned to the nest.

Birds of prey are especially noted for doing away with weak or ailing siblings. "Survival of the fittest" it is called: the healthiest of the nestlings are able to monopolize the food brought by their parents and soon outmuscle their weaker nestmates. The weak die, either from starvation or outright fratricide.

Weak hawk and owl nestlings are also sometimes the victims of Kronism, slain and eaten by their own parents just as the Greek god Kronos swallowed his first five children, fearful that they would usurp his power. Kronism is rare and usually occurs only during times of especially harsh weather when parent birds cannot find sufficient quantities of food to sustain their entire brood.

But it does happen and it does arouse revulsion among human observers who apply their human standards to situations that are essentially beyond the grasp of human ethics. Too soon we forget the horrifying tales of Kronism among our own kind, acts committed by persons driven to desperate madness by the ravages of war, famine or insanity. Perhaps our historic ability to engage in such acts has nothing to do with madness. Perhaps it is an echo of ties to other times, other creatures and other, baser instincts.

It is an unnerving thought.

The wayward nestling slipped from my hands into the nest and immediately pushed itself into the mass of familiar down that was its brothers and sisters. The board was tapped back into place and Matt and I left the barn, wondering if the bird would ever hover the air above the field across the road or know the rigors of raising its own young.

The bird has not reappeared in the weeds below the nest and the parents still attend their young. I am sorely tempted to pry off the board again to see if there are still four young in the nest. But I am more concerned that the nest — and however many young it holds — not be further disturbed, threatening the welfare of the entire brood.

The bird's chances are not good, but we wish it well.

* * *

Doug Jones

Six weeks until the first frost?

The goldenrod in the clearing beside the barn has been in bloom for several days now and that, according to folk tradition, means we have but six more weeks òf frost-free nights. Preposterous as that may seem as we swing from July to August, there are indeed signs of impending autumn throughout the land.

The first solitary sandpiper whistled down upon the dark mud of the larger pond last week, pausing for a day or two on its southward trek to dine on tadpoles, water beetles and other delicacies. Its preference for solitude befits its name and there is something about things solitary that befits the approach of autumn, a time for reflection and self-assessment.

Summer's hottest days are August-borne, but the evenings now and then bring a hint of autumn's chill. Heat waves are common, but cold snaps are not to be discounted. Hurricane-time is near.

The black-eyed Susans have been a part of the back forty colorscape for weeks and are beginning to curl and brown. The daisies are long-gone, except for a few widely scattered stragglers, stunted as though ashamed of such woeful truancy.

Even some of the hardwood trees show signs of changing color. The diseased, overcrowded and aged are the first to wrap their veins with whispers of yellow and red, though another eight weeks or so will pass before the change begins in earnest.

The raspberries have long been picked and the blueberries are beckoning thrushes and thrashers. The wild grapes are purpling ever so slightly. Tadpoles have found legs and some have mastered the use of their new limbs in concert with the disappearance of now useless tails. The ponds and bogs are quieter now as the season's young become learnéd in the ways of stealth and deception.

The winds have changed, too. They blow strangely in the evening now, pushing before them shocks of dried grass that crackle underfoot.

Butterflies are everywhere; not the dainty ones of spring and early summer, but the larger fritillaries and monarchs of summer's eve. The black-banded, orange monarchs have sought out the milkweed patches to deposit their eggs, trusting the remnants of the season to be kind to their offspring who yet must evolve from egg to adult and fly thousands of miles to the winterless South.

Summer's birds have fledged and birdwatchers puzzle anew over the transitional plummage arrayed before them: sparrows look more alike than ever, warblers are brown where they should be yellow. . . . A pair of robins has fledged its second brood in a

Maine Fish & Game Dept.

spruce tree along the ridge trail and the tree swallows left their nesting boxes scattered along the woods road three weeks ago.

There is one bird whose domestic chores have just begun. The goldfinch awaits the blooming of the thistle to rear its young, using the soft, cotton-like blossom to line its nest. I assume the similar dandelion blossoms of spring are too short or too stiff for its purposes. The thistles have begun to bloom.

Tracks in the soft earth of the woods road and the path to the beech grove indicate that this year's fawns are now accompanying their parents constantly. Successive broods of muskrats have overcrowded the larger pond and individuals can occasionally be seen hunching with comical but admirable determination across the dry woods floor in search of their own domains. Meanwhile, evaporation and seepage have taken their toll on the ponds, now roughly one-third their springtime dimensions and rife with algae.

Mushrooms, irrefutable evidence of autumn's approach, pierce the matted pine needles and hardwood leaves with muted browns, brilliant oranges and vibrant reds.

Crickets are everywhere, squeezing through cracks in the granite block foundation of the farmhouse to fill the kitchen with their distinctively late-summer "song," surprising uninitiated visitors with their sudden, bouncing forays across the floor. Outside, their grasshopper kin launch by the dozens from the dry grass and patches of gravel we optimistically call a "lawn."

It is a time of transition, different from any other day or week of the year only in the tenor of its voice and the hue of its garb. No day or moment is divorced from the motion to and from transition. Even if our planet were to utterly vanish from the cosmos, the pendulum would still swing and somewhere, no doubt, a yellow leaf would flutter downward and a cricket would rub one knee against the other and pay homage to approaching autumn.

* * *

As the lush tangle of summer yields to the brown-gray tangle of autumn, the shapes of things become more obvious and more astonishing. There is also reassurance to be found in the re-emerging shapes, testimony to the unity of the world's countless elements.

Steve calls it "Pigtail Bend," a sharp curve in one of the woodlot trails where a 10-foot pine struggles to survive in the shadows of its elders. It is no ordinary tree, this teen-aged fighter, for its trunk executes a perfect, 360-degree twist starting about one foot above the ground. It does indeed look like a pig's tail and while Steve and I wonder at its cause, David insists it stands as mute but firm proof of the "cosmic spiral" of nature.

He may have something there.

The cause of the tree's unusual configuration is fairly certain: a heavy branch or other object fell upon it some years ago, pushing the young and supple trunk downward and forcing subsequent growth to twist around the object toward the sunlight. The object has since rotted away, leaving only its eye-catching and thought-provoking product.

Although there is a reasonable explanation to this particular phenomenon, it is nonetheless one of innumerable examples of David's "cosmic spiral." I think my fellow woods wanderer's phrase could easily be translated into such terms as "unity" and "truth."

The truth of the matter is that we and all the Earth's elements are united by certain common denominators, the most obvious and significant being our presence on the same planet. Common forces — gravity, for one — cast us in a common mold.

Just as a flower opens to capture the sun's rays, so a human stretches her or his form across the sand to warm the skin. The bark of trees expands and cracks; human skin, too, cracks and falls imperceptibly away. Robbed of light and air, both the human and the mosquito perish.

The Earth turns, the moon passes and all things take note of the motion. The oceans heave. Plates of rock grate one against the other. Mountains crack. Winds blow, pushing rain-filled clouds. Streams flow. Roots penetrate the soil. Petals unfold. Stems bend to follow the sun. Butterflies move from blossom to blossom, morning to evening, spring to fall.

Deep within the shadowy hemlock grove, mosses gather to carpet the rocks and damp logs. Lowering my face to within inches of the tight, green mass, I see not the moss but an entire forest. Several hundred feet overhead, a hawk wheels in purposeful circles, scanning a forest through which a myriad of creatures roam, among them a two-legged one bent curiously over a patch of moss.

In the midst of a small, lively stream squats a rock about which clings a ring of grassy earth. Crawling, tumbling and burrowing about the island are nameless, tiny creatures, many of which no doubt spend all their brief lives on the water-washed continent. Australia is different only in human terms, its 'roos and wombats merely more substantial than those which eke out a living on the islet in the stream.

A moth clings to the smooth surface of a pruning scar on a pine tree, its wings firmly covering a cascade of brownish eggs that spill from its twitching abdomen. Two dozen feet above, the remnants of a warbler's nest sway gently in the breeze. How different, really, are the two?

At the edge of a nearby woodlot, a host of tiny insects decimates a gnarled cherry tree. One hundred yards away, a logging crew noisily goes about its business of stripping the land.

And a miniscule human returns to his miniscule dwelling that clings to the surface of a dust mote whispering through space.

* * *

An eagle soaring effortlessly against the deep blue of a summer sky, ascending the invisible rungs of a thermal "ladder," is an awesome sight, the epitome of the hypnotic influence flight exerts on earth-bound humans.

Humans have yearned to fly as long as there have been humans and the longing has consistently been integrated into our various modes of worship. Angels have wings, as did members of the Egyptian, Greek and Roman pantheons of gods (most who did not have wings could nonetheless fly). Many American Indians worshipped the eagle and the hawk and adorned themselves with their feathers, the choicest often being reserved for the tribal shaman.

Diminish a person's inhibitions and sensibilities, as with drugs or alcohol, and you just may see someone try to fly ... with disasterous, gory results.

We have tried for centuries to mimic the eagle, covering our bodies with wax and feathers, strapping ungainly wooden wings to our arms, tying hapless birds to baskets and bicycles, propelling ourselves skyward astraddle monstrous engines. Many a child is familiar with the consequences of trusting an umbrella to provide a gentle descent from garage roof to ground.

Until the day we are born with hollow bones, very different muscles and, of course, feathers, we cannot hope to achieve unassisted flight. For the time being, we must content ourselves with hang gliders, Cessnas, balloons, rockets and 747s.

The bird, you see, is a marvel of specialization that cannot be duplicated with wire, wood, metal or even the most exotic of alloys.

The bones of a bird are extremely thin when compared to those of a human and the longer of its bones are hollow, thereby decreasing its body weight. The bones are joined by a complex net-

Bald Eagle   Irene Vandermolen

work of incredibly responsive muscles that may constitute more than half of its total weight.

The bones and muscles provide the framework for the greatest wonder of all, the feathers.

Feathers are obviously a bird's principal feature, the evolutionary offspring of reptilian scales. The feathers of any given bird, with the exception of the oddly flightless few, are very specific in their appointed flight functions. The wings bear the longer and stronger feathers required for flight, the primaries fanning outward from what is the bird's equivalent of the human hand, the secondaries extending backward from its version of our forearm.

Among the owls, those masters of virtually noiseless night flight, the feathers are extraordinarily specialized, covered with a velvet-like fluff that muffles noise. How else could such a bird descend upon a mouse that dies without hearing a sound?

Some waterfowl may carry as many as 12,000 feathers, small warblers up to 3,000, but each is as marvelous as the whole. The wing, back, head, tail and chest feathers of most birds have what can best be described as tiny hooks which permit one feather to be

Ruffed Grouse

held tightly against another. The more compressed a bird's feathers, the greater its streamlining, the lesser its wind resistance.

Very basically speaking, a bird flies because the air pressure atop its wings is less than the pressure below its wings. That arrangement, which produces what is known as "lift," is created by the bird's wing motion: the air traveling across the tops of its wings moves faster than the air traveling across their undersides.

Upon close examination, a bird's wing motion is very simple. Tracing a figure-eight pattern in the air, its wingtips open on the upstroke, seemingly gripping the air, and flatten or compress on the downstroke, accelerating the rate at which the air travels across the tops of its wings. Birds do not, in other words, "flap" their wings. The pattern of a bird's wing stroke has been aptly likened to the butterfly stroke in swimming. If a bird did "flap" its wings in an up-and-down fashion, it would get nowhere, just as the swimmer treading water with such an arm motion remains relatively stationary.

The coordination of muscle, bone, feather and eye is uncanny. One has only to watch a large hawk zip effortlessly through a grove of tightly enmeshed trees to appreciate the coordination of its physical elements. To achieve a comparable feat, a human would have to pilot a single-engine airplane through a redwood forest . . . below treetop level. But the fact remains that a human foolish enough to try such a stunt would be relying on considerably more than her or his own physical resources: the bird does it on its own.

That is the way it will always be, unless God or natural selection intervenes. We may fleetingly sense the ecstasy of flight from a hang glider or a parasail, but the flight of the bird is beyond our grasp.

The autumn migration has begun in earnest, though the season has not quite arrived. The forests, fields and mountains are bidding adieu to their complement of warblers, thrushes, ducks and other sundry birds, now south-bound in pursuit of the retreating warmth.

It is a mysterious, awesome occurrence, this migration. No one really knows how or why birds migrate. They fly, of course, and it is easy enough to say that their flights are motivated by the approach or retreat of winter. But that is not enough.

There are nearly as many theories on the nature and means of migratory behavior as there are species of birds that migrate. No one theory enjoys a clear majority of support within the scientific community.

There are those who contend that birds migrate according to the availability of necessary food resources. That is probably true, but why do they not stay put when they find a locale that suits their needs? Why fly north from comparatively food-rich Georgia or Alabama to nest in Labrador?

In answer to that apparently self-refuting contradiction, some ornithologists argue that migratory birds are heeding a "clock" set in motion during the glacial eras of prehistory. These theorists feel that birds which now fly north in the spring to nest once were nonmigratory residents of their present breeding ranges, forced south by the advancing ice sheets and still heeding the impulse to return each year to their natural "homes."

Others say overpopulation dictates migration, a theory that can be at least partially tied to the glacial-migration argument. It is reasonable to assume that the retreat of the glaciers thousands of years ago led to a warming of the continent, a quantitative increase in the displaced birds and the need to expand their ranges . . . northward.

Canada Geese (center)   John Snow

Guy Gannett Publishing Co.

But how do they do it?

Because the vast majority of migratory birds follow very specific "flyways" or routes on their journeys, a great many researchers are convinced that they use natural landmarks as guides. It has, in fact, been more than adequately demonstrated that birds do follow certain rivers, mountain ranges and coastlines. But most birds migrate at night after having rested and gorged themselves during the daylight hours, and they can hardly see such features from altitudes of anywhere from a few score to several thousands of feet.

Do they perhaps navigate by the stars, as did our ancient mariners? Yes. At least some birds can do so, a fact that has been proven by releasing mid-migration birds in planetariums where they doggedly follow precise stellar maps, even when their "target" stars are repositioned to negate the effectiveness of any other directional senses they may employ.

But many birds ignore foul weather to continue their migratory flights, some launching out across vast stretches of ocean while clouds obscure whatever stellar maps they may have etched on their instinct. Even the tiny hummingbird can tackle the Gulf of Mexico, reaching its Central and South American destinations with uncanny accuracy in foul weather. Such birds have no stars, mountains or rivers to follow.

Some researchers argue rather convincingly that birds are capable of "seeing" land features — and of judging the positions and distances of land masses when flying over open water — by comparing and analyzing such factors as air currents, temperatures, thermal pressures and humidity. The soaring birds, notably the hawks and albatrosses, are deft at the use of thermals and it is reasonable to assume that all birds have some comprehension of those and other atmospheric phenomena and conditions. Humans, after all, know something of house construction methods because they live in houses. Atmospheric conditions would serve as good guideposts, bred as they are by our planet's physical constitution, the shape and location of its oceans and continents and the meanderings of its rivers and mountain ranges.

It is quite possible that birds possess atmospheric "gauges" far superior to our own mechanical instruments, capable of performing the same and other, unknown functions with greater speed and accuracy.

Each of these and numerous other theories has merit and it may be that birds use whichever mechanism suits their needs. It is also quite possible that we will never know exactly how they do it.

Isabel Lewando

AUTUMN

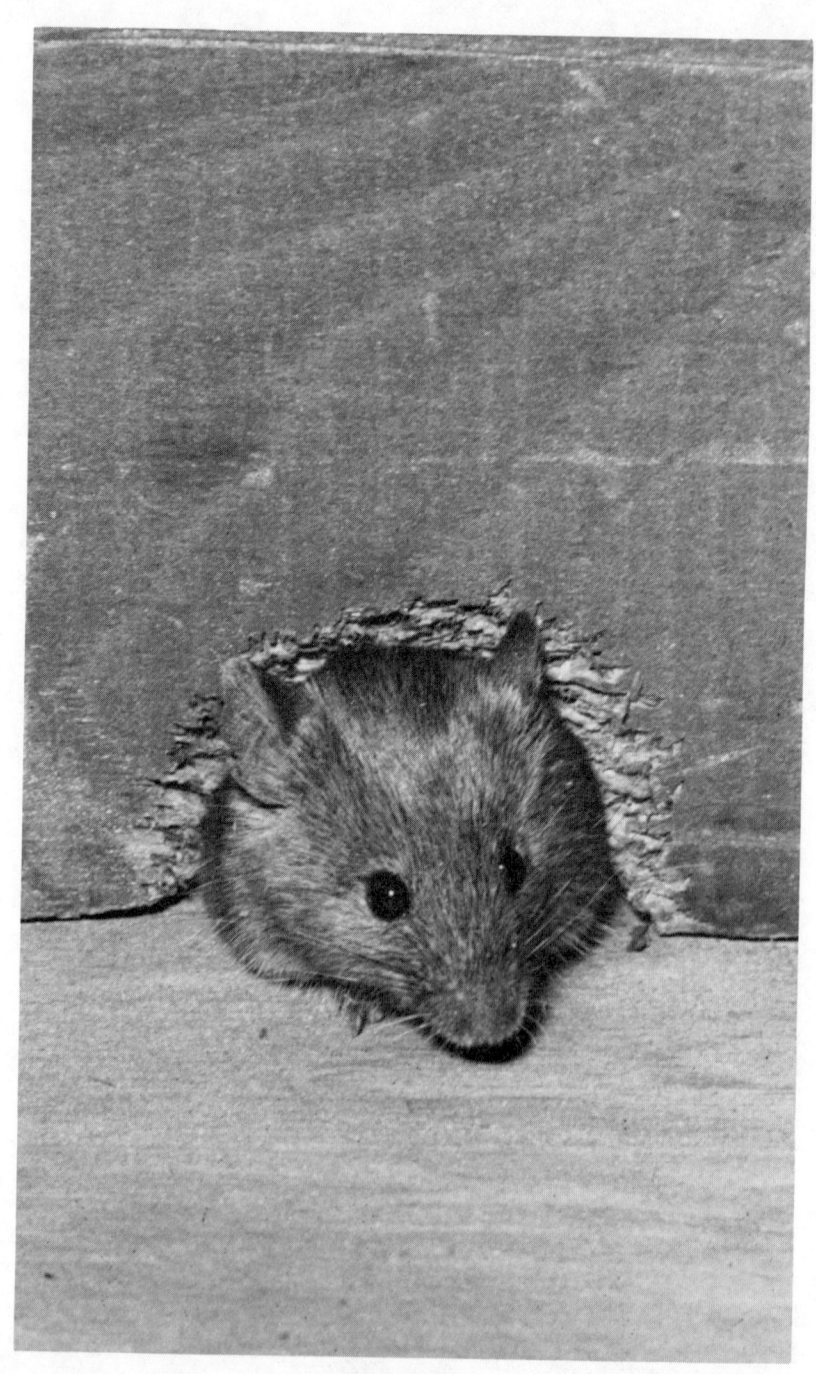

House Mouse   Leonard Lee Rue III

BRIGHT & DULL

The furry little monsters are back!

I'm talking about the mice, of course, the smallest creatures known to wear army boots.

Actually, they have never been gone and they certainly do not wear boots of any kind. Heck, they can't button their shirts, so how do you expect them to lace up their boots?

Regardless of the facts, it does seem that they have been gone for a while and it does seem that they have finally learned the fine art of boot lacing.

If you do not count the noises produced by toys purchased in fits of idiocy to quiet noisy kids, the farmhouse had been reasonably tranquil throughout the summer months. It always seems so after the mice pack up and head for their summer cottages in the woodpile and bramble thicket.

But they're coming back! I had hoped they would lose their way or fall in love with the resident woodpile and thicket mice, but those sorts of breaks seldom come my way. Well, some of them did fall in love during their summer vacations, but they have brought their new mates with them to the farmhouse.

I can hear them now, out behind the stacked maple and birch, getting ready for the trek to their winter quarters.

"Rodney, dearest, I simply cannot spend the winter in this filthy woodpile! I'm going home to the house, so you'll have to choose between me and the woodpile."

"Yes, my little cheesecake. But mother can't stay here all alone. She'll have to come, too."

"In that case, we'd better invite widow Nibble. I will not spend all my days fawning over your mother!"

And so it goes. Widow Nibble, naturally, cannot leave her niece Gertrude for the entire winter and Gertrude gets hives if she cannot be near Brown Bart and he is lost without his Uncle Portwine and. . . .

So they all come, squeezing through the cracks and the crevices with all their baggage. And their boots.

Now, people will tell you that a mouse is a quiet creature, but when you are trying to sleep they are about as silent as a railroad switching yard.

They don't scamper or skitter. They stomp.

They don't squeak or squeal. They scream.

They don't sip or sample. They slobber.

They don't even court quietly, preferring chases and chokeholds to sedate encounters and tenderness. I suppose, though, that if I had such a short life expectancy I would be out there chasing and grabbing. Go for it, Gertrude!

I also suppose that I cannot fault the little perishers for liking the farmhouse as much as they do. It is a fairly nice place, filled with niches, goodies and warmth. There is not much wind and hardly any snow. The dog and the cats are too stupid and preoccupied with one another to worry about.

But . . . do they have to bring their boots?

* * *

Lodged against the exterior window molding with its legs drawn up against its body, the brown-gray object looked more like an over-ripe grape than a spider.

But a spider it was. Not just "a" spider, but one of the biggest the farmhouse or barn had disclosed for years. Its abdomen was the size of a quarter and its eyes, leg hairs and "fangs" were plainly visible. Had it been on the inside of the window, I might have thought twice about allowing it to stay: more than one bedroom-roaming spider has learned just how heavy my boots are, if indeed anything can learn anything in a split second.

But because it was outside and because it demonstrated a voracious appetite for houseflies, earwigs and deer flies, it was permitted to maintain its lease.

Furthermore, its location on just the other side of the glass means it can be readily observed. It has become a captivating object of study for the boys . . . and for any adults who care about such things. Nephew R.J., for one, was speechless (for a few record-setting seconds, anyway) to learn with his own eyes that some spiders will wrap their prey for storage and later consumption. I do not think his mother was terribly interested in his detailed account of the procedure, though, and deftly ignored his appeals to "come look at it suck the guts outta this bug."

Those who do take the time to really watch a spider are more apt to be amazed than distressed, for the spider is a phenomenal and entertaining creature. Spiders are neither devils nor demons. Neither are they insects. They are arachnids, eight-legged and wingless specialists with their own evolutionary pedigree and future. Scorpions, mites and ticks are also arachnids.

They range in size from the huge tarantulas of South America,

Charles H. Merrill

Guy Gannett Publishing Co.

which have been known to stretch a foot from the tip of one leg to the tip of an opposing leg, to several miniscule spiders less than one-fiftieth of an inch in diameter.

Their habits and habitats are equally diverse. Some spin webs to ensnare their prey while others are active hunters and still others prefer the stealth of the ambush. A few seek their meals under water, carrying with them a bubble of air to provide buoyancy and oxygen to breathe. One variety even slings a sticky ball at its prey.

All spiders are equipped with two chelicerae, bulbous protrusions just above the mouth, with which to grasp their prey. Each chelicera is tipped with a sharp "fang" through which the spider can secrete a poison into the body of its victim. Only a very few are poisonous to humans, however, and those do not bite unless given cause to do so. The poison employed by spiders is usually meant to paralyze, but in some cases it is designed to kill.

Prey immobilization is a horrible-sounding but consummately ingenious method of preserving a meal until it is needed. Spoilage is eliminated because the victim is still alive, a fact which humans who detest rancid meat and moldy jam should appreciate.

Humans should also appreciate the spider as a natural and effective control mechanism. Imagine, if you can, how the even less savory creatures of the world — mosquitoes, deer flies and tsetse flies, to name but a few — would fare if their numbers were not kept constantly in check by the spiders.

Spiders are not so bad after all. They may not be cuddly or cute, but they are worth their weight in dead bugs, if not in gold.

*   *   *

Matt and Josh are getting older and more venturesome every day. The "older" does not bother me too much, but their increasingly venturesome nature sometimes spawns outlandish fears.

Kids like to explore and the back forty must be about as enticing to them as the Orient was to Marco Polo. They want to know its every crevice, ridge and bower, from the roadway to well beyond the "back path" logging road that currently represents the limit of their unsupervised expeditions.

They trudge the two acres within their appointed "wilderness" with the impatience of bears at a beehive, yearning to plunge into the mysterious territory beyond.

"We forgot" is the explanation offered on those few occasions when they have yielded to that temptation. The consequences of such forgetfulness need not be mentioned here, but they have

Guy Gannett Publishing Co.

been swift and sure, fueled by such fears as all parents entertain.

Few crises arouse as much publicity and hair-tearing as children lost in the woods. Such crises are all too often very real, but it is always "the other family" whose children have been missing for three days in what the network newspeople describe as "the trackless forests" of somewhere.

Those of us who are parents know the fear.

The fear can be eased considerably, however, by instilling in our children a respect for the woods that makes the associated rules of conduct sensible and palatable. If we know that they know how to act in the woods, we will not worry quite so much. They can be trusted, if they are given the proper tools to work with. The most important of the tools are understanding and experience, sprinkled with a dash of parental patience.

No child, regardless of his or her intelligence, is going to know what to do in the woods — or anywhere else, for that matter — without having some understanding of its character and nuances. The woods can be a terrifying place to the newcomer, especially the newcomer tender in years. Understanding comes with familiarity.

Matt and Josh have the run of the front two acres of the back forty, an ideal "boot camp" of sorts that embraces the smaller of the two ponds, a pine grove, a few glacial boulders, thickets and that section of the "back path" that is best for bicycle riding. Within those precise borders, the boys can learn for themselves the sounds, smells and textures of the land and its parts. They learn such elemental but important things as how to negotiate a steep embankment and how to tell a weak tree limb from a strong one.

Of course, no one is going to push young children out the back door and tell them to "go spend a few hours learning about the woods." That sort of approach may create needless fears that a youngster can nurture for the remainder of his or her life, fears that can weave horrifying scenarios of frothing wolves, gargantuan serpents and mad hermits.

Before a youngster can go it alone, even on a very limited scale, he or she must be given some basic rules and demonstrate both a willingness and an ability to employ common sense. Call it "responsibility" if you will.

Matt and Josh have the geographic boundaries of the two-acre "boot camp" to honor, as well as a number of behavioral edicts. They know not to bother any animals and that if they should encounter one that is acting at all strangely to walk slowly and calmly away. They know not to eat any of the many wild berries and fruits unless a knowledgeable adult says they may. They know to stay put if they are at all confused about where they are. They know, I think, more than I give them credit for.

Because the boys are of different ages — Matt is 10, Josh 6 — the rules vary a bit for each. Josh is not permitted to venture to the far corners of the "boot camp" alone and we tend to look the other way when Matt pushes its borders a few yards deeper into the woods.

Different kinds of borders are being extended, in fact, as they learn more about themselves and the woods ... and as Judy and I learn to trust their intelligence and abilities.

But it is hard. It is part of letting go, of watching them literally walk away, self-reliant and sure, less and less tied to our knowledge and judgments. I keep telling myself not to worry and one day I may listen to my advice. Probably not, though.

* * *

The landscape is again vibrating with the brilliant colors of autumn, a magical time which we dutifully observe but seldom try to understand.

We take it for granted that the maples will turn red and the poplars yellow. It is a rare person who pauses to wonder why, although the explanation is every bit as intriguing as its visual reality.

As school children, we all learned about chlorophyll and its role in photosynthesis, the greening of plants and the production of oxygen. It is the loss of chlorophyll which spurs the dramatic color changes in our trees.

Chlorophyll is to be found in the chloroplasts which surround each vein in each leaf. As summer turns to autumn, a small, corklike ring at the base of each leaf's stem begins to harden and tighten, slowly damming the flow of liquid nutrients to the leaf and its chloroplasts.

As the leaf's circulation is decreased, its chloroplasts and chlorophyll begin to break down, rather like a cube of sugar in a cup of hot coffee. Instead of producing a colorless leaf, the process permits one of three principal color pigments to emerge, pigments which had been present throughout the summer but which lacked the strength to supercede or subdue the green of the chlorophyll. Carotene, for example, is the pigment which gives both carrots their orange hue and maples their cloaks of reddish-orange. Xan-

Maine Development Commission

thophyll creates the bright yellow of the autumn birches and poplars while anthocyanin causes the leaves of the dogwood to turn purple.

Even after the leaf has adopted its proper autumn color and its circulation has been utterly terminated, the cork-like ring at its base continues to contract. Eventually it tightens enough to allow the leaf to be plucked from its place by a gentle breeze.

Once on the ground, the leaf is subjected to the rotting influences of the autumn drizzle and the following spring's rainfall and snowmelt. Just as its chloroplasts were broken down by the halt of circulation within the leaf, so the leaf itself is broken down into its basic chemical elements, some of which may well nurture the next generation of leaves.

We have rightfully attached great significance to our trees, both commercial and otherwise. We see in their life cycles a hint of reincarnation and resurrection and those who find solace in such potentials regard the tree with emotions akin to reverence.

Trees have played major roles in this country's folklore, too. Consider George Washington and his father's cherry tree. Or Johnny Appleseed. Or Paul Bunyan.

There are socio-religious trees of Life, Wisdom and Heaven. It was Matthew who said that "the tree is known by its fruit" and Joyce Kilmer who coined the phrase "lovely as a tree."

Is it really coincidental that our family pedigrees are known as "trees" and that in tracing that pedigree we examine our "roots." If you happen to be a bit flaky, you sometimes are said to be "out of your tree" and if you are venturesome you may go "out on a limb."

It was the fruit of the apple tree that got us where we are today.

Wordsworth perhaps expressed the value of the tree most eloquently: "One impulse from a vernal wood may teach you more of man, of moral evil and of good, than all the sages can."

But it is our children, those tree-climbing, treehouse-building innocents, who are probably most attuned to our fascination with trees. They, more than we, can feel the ghostly brushing of a leaf against the hairy cheek of some nameless ancestor whose feet seldom touched the ground.

* * *

The fog slithered between the belly of the small airplane and ocean, erasing all sense of direction and motion. Only pressure-flattened ribbons of water on the windshield and blind faith in the "laws" of nature and mechanics provided assurance that we were still aloft and moving.

The fog-out was brief. Within a minute the sheets of fog dissipated into shreds of scudding mist. The isles and shoals of Penobscot Bay were spread below us like jewels upon a gray metal table.

Matt had never flown before, a fact betrayed by his wide-eyed, open-mouthed excitement. If there had been more time to prepare for the flight, perhaps he would have allowed excitement to yield to fear. But Herb had made a quick telephone call to North Haven from his Owls Head office, found the conditions on the island "marginal" and hurriedly squeezed the three of us into his plane to "give it a try." There simply was no time to think, let alone worry.

At mid-runway, Judy pointed to the tape holding her passenger window together and grimaced.

One must go aloft in a small plane to fully appreciate the relationships between land, water, temperature, wind and motion. On this particular day, the wind was gusting and eddying with confusing strength, bouncing the plane every which-way. But there was constancy amid the confusion: the pressures and currents over land and water varied significantly and predictably.

Over open water, the plane moved with relative ease and smoothness, but the slightest cluster of islands meant a jarring bounce, dip and shudder. It was somewhat gratifying, in a smug sort of way, to learn later that several of the friends we were to meet on North Haven were at that moment having a green-faced ride below us on the ferry out of Rockland.

The disjointed elements of land and sea assume a singular character when viewed from aloft. Islands become not separate entities, but segments of a melodic whole, their submerged flanks visible as rings of green, blue and brown, descending to a common, unseen floor.

That common floor is shared by all, giving life and sustenance to countless living things within and without the water, rising to heights beyond the reach of wave and spray. There, rising farther still, hills and mountains recline across the horizon, islands in a long-ago yesterday and, perhaps, in a distant tomorrow.

Small as eider ducks seen from shore, boats in search of lobster, hake and haddock plied the gray waters, their wakes lost in the chaos of wave and wind.

Banking sharply, Herb jockeyed the plane for the approach to the grass airstrip stretching across the ancient pastureland of the

Guy Gannett Publishing Co.

Ambassador Thomas J. Watson estate, an oasis that has catered to the likes of Charles Lindberg and Thailand's King Bhumibol and Queen Sirikit. The plane's nose seemed to point straight down toward the massed rocks of the shoreline.

The land grew rapidly closer as the plane shuddered and bounced through layer upon layer of air, turning the sharply defined tones of mid-October trees into a blur of dull brown. Pebbles became boulders. Huge trees emerged from the blankets of yellow, green, red and brown.

Suddenly, the crowns of the trees were above us and the green swath of the runway was racing past, its blur echoing the quickly fading ecstasy of a new perspective on familiar sights.

* * *

The afternoon breezes whisper impatiently through the pine grove, bearing brown pine needles and the brittle wings of dead moths.

Gripped by burdock nettles, clusters of dry grass scuttle across the lawn to settle in the lee of the groaning barn. There, the vegetable matter will disintegrate, scattering its nutrient soul across the chilling earth to sustain its progeny on their journeys from spring to autumn.

Another summer has come and gone; autumn slips away. Winter approaches in the shadow of that nameless season of barren trees and frosty earth.

It is, poets and other weavers of metaphors tell us, a time of death, a time when life congeals in the silent recesses of the mind's impatience. It is a time for impatience, but hardly for death.

The cosmic clock seems to pause for an agonizing eon, lost in some limbo between late afternoon and midnight. Its ticking, so reassuring in the noontime of the year, is muffled and sometimes drowned by the chill wind. Its hour-hand seems to tire beneath its own weight.

But the hand does move — if only when we are looking the other way — and creeps inexorably toward midnight. We find ourselves looking not at the hand, but at its midnight destination. We perceive finality in the hour and shiver slightly as a cold wind pushes beneath the door to lace the pendulum with frost.

The hour-hand will indeed reach midnight and winter's snows will indeed come.

Listen closely, though, at the midnight hour. "Tick...tock." The

Jim Daniels

pendulum will not cease its appointed journey and midnight will pass as quickly as it came.

The snows will deepen and the ice will thicken. But the pendulum will continue to move, pushing the hour-hand ever downward toward the crocus-colored dawn. Whispers unlike those of evening will ride the swirling breezes, promises pantomimed in frost.

And then the dawn will come, washing the sky with warm pinks and golds. With the labored protestations of an arthritic, the cold fingers of midnight will withdraw from the earth. The leaves of evening piled high in the lee of the barn will resume their transformation, their skeletons pierced by the tentative shoots of burrdock.

And the pendulum will move . . . .

The evening hour is the bleakest time of year, but it is a time that I have come to love because it lays bare the footprints of summer and amplifies the whisper of seasons yet to come.

We forget on our journey from here to there that the disappearance of one time or thing lends visibility and voice to other times and things. Or perhaps it is because we make that journey, bounded by birth and death, that we place rigid limits on all that we see and hear.

All things transitory are vehemently denied by the din and demand of clocks, calendars and appointment books.

If this is Sunday, tomorrow must be Monday.

But the back forty and its kin speak eloquently — to those who will listen — of timelessness, of entwining death and resurrection. Late fall is indeed a bleak season, to those who see without examining and listen without hearing, for people whose minds and wristwatches have become synchronized.

Late fall is the time of year in which to marvel at the world's simplest perfections, those shielded or muted throughout the immediately bygone months by grander sights.

A mud-and-twig robin's nest clings to the crotch of a small elm behind the barn, slowly disintegrating in the damp chill, tenacious proof of its maker's engineering skills. How often had I braced myself on those very limbs while stretching into the raspberry patch? Had the young birds trembled in silent dread?

A fox pads noiselessly through the bushes bordering the large pond, probing each tuft of grass and other likely rodent shelter with its nose. How often had it watched my summer passings, hidden by the leaves that now moulder on the dank earth?

The fallen leaves themselves testify to the timelessness of this and all seasons. It has been a week or more since the last completed its trek from twig to ground, but already its thinner portions have yielded to the onslaught of frosty dampness. A mere skeleton of veins remains, though it, too, soon will dissipate to sustain the tree from which it fell.

How many times, I wonder, might a single molecule repeat the journey from leaf to ground and back to leaf?

There is change, yes, but no ending. And no perceptible beginning.

The land itself becomes the soloist in this most natural of symphonies, unchallenged by the greenery of summer or the reds and oranges of earlier fall. Its every nuance is bared: here it rises steeply through the beech grove; there it descends abruptly into the dark hemlocks. Each crease and wrinkle echoes its infancy and its age.

Mosses and lichens that have clung throughout the summer to rocks and aged logs now add their hues to the composition. Ear to the ground, I can almost hear the warmth of summer slipping deeper into the mantle of rock, roots withdrawing their tendrils from the biting air and countless creatures twitching in the first throes of wintersleep.

All the world is washed with gray and the simplest shred of color — a feather discarded by a passing jay or a mat of green moss — burns like an ember in the darkest night. Earth and air become one, joined by the placenta-like lace of the bare treetops.

This is the time to sit, alone and silently, in the lee of a rock and listen to the passing of time. It moves noisily through the barren trees, rattling as it goes, sending brittle leaves scurrying down the ridge. It alternately shrieks, moans, chuckles and howls. And now and then it pauses to whisper gently of its past and future visitations.

It has nothing to say of beginnings and ends.

Empty and broken, they dot the bushes along the pathways and tote roads, trembling in the wind.

They are the nests of birds now gone, shabby-looking dishes and bowls from which noisily uncertain grackles, warblers and vireos were fledged a few short weeks ago.

At about this time each year, I conduct a mental "nest census," marveling anew over the fact that so many could go undetected for so long. During the verdant months of one summer, I pinpointed the locations of four grackle and red-winged blackbird

Isabel Lewando

nests in the large pond, only to discover 17 after the leaves had fallen and the waters retreated. Twelve of those were unquestionably of that season's vintage, five possible survivors from the preceding summer.

Summer's leaves and grasses keep much from the eyes of even the most diligent observer. The weeks from leaf-drop to Christmas are the time in which to learn just how limited one's perceptions really are.

There is a new muskrat lodge in the center of the large pond, a heap of sticks and mud that brings to three the total number of the animals' domiciles. Nine nests this year; grackle, blackbird and blue jay. A single, abandoned egg sits in a corner of the duck box. Insect egg cases hug the bare branches of the bushes, waiting the warmth of April. Sluggish beetles and spiders crowd the cracks and shadows of bough and rock.

The nests, however, are the most captivating.

One need only to disassemble a bird's nest to truly appreciate the genius and talent of its builder. Better still, try taking it apart one stick at a time, without dislodging adjoining sticks or strands of fiber. It is possible, but very frustrating, perhaps even humiliating to a human convinced of his or her own mechanical superiority.

If you do decide to give it a try, equip yourself with a pair of tweezers, some toothpicks and several sheets of white paper. Use the tweezers to gently pull materials from the nest, aided at times by the toothpicks which can be used as miniature pry-bars and probes. Sort the construction materials on the sheets of paper, each sheet reserved for a specific type of material. A jar of water with a misting nozzle can prove helpful if the nest is "glued" together with mud: a light spraying of a hardened area will usually loosen the material. (The real challenge, however, is to use tweezers and toothpicks to loosen and remove each pellet or piece of mud separately.)

A count of the materials coaxed from a nest does not provide an accurate gauge of the number of trips made by its builder during the construction process, for many pieces are dropped or discarded. Furthermore, only the experienced and well-equipped scientist can determine how much saliva, spider web, caterpiller "silk" and other hard-to-detect materials were used.

Anyone contemplating such an experiment should be wary of bird parasites, particularly lice, that may infest a nest for a time after its occupants have left. A few quick sprays with an insecticide should do the trick, but I prefer to smoke them out over an

Guy Gannett Publishing Co.

Guy Gannett Publishing Co.

outdoor fire smothered momentarily with green leaves or weeds.

It is wise to avoid stripping an area of its seemingly empty and useless nests. Abandoned nests are utilized by a variety of animals, including small rodents and resident birds, for winter roosts, feeding platforms and even homes. The larger nests of crows and hawks are frequently claimed by owls and squirrels.

Birds use a wide array of things, some of them quite bizarre, in the construction of their nests. Bald eagles have been known to use tin cans, boots, garbage bags, small buoys and even empty shotgun shells, a telling adaptation of human trash. Some flycatchers invariably add a snake skin to their nests, perhaps with the misguided conviction that it will deter predators. Orioles, whose nests hang from the outermost branches of lofty hardwood

Guy Gannett Publishing Co.

trees, are more concerned with inaccessibility than invisibility and therefore will often use brightly colored yarn and string.

A catbird nest in one of the hydrangeas at the front of the farmhouse this year contained strips of cellophane, string, bits of paper and one rubber band. Befitting their size, hummingbirds use bits of lichen and spider webs.

Perhaps the most unusual nests of all are those of the swifts of Southeast Asia. Using plenty of saliva, they attach their domiciles to the walls of caves. The caves are leased to "nest farmers" who harvest the nests with the precision and care of a Midwestern wheat farmer, selling them to restaurants which turn them into bird's nest soup. That misunderstood delicacy is, in reality, bird spit.

Winter-Garbed Weasel   Irene Vandermolen

BEASTS OF THE FROST

Watching a carnivore stalk and kill its prey can be an unnerving experience. If the carnivore is a weasel, you will not soon forget the sight.

Moving with almost complete silence and utilizing a sense of smell unparalleled on the back forty, the weasel tackles most anything its own size and a number of creatures of far greater bulk. It is the animal's method of killing that captures the attention.

With a leap as silent as its tread, the weasel grasps its prey and plunges its needle-sharp teeth into its neck, severing the spinal column at the base of the skull with a quickness and dexterity many a surgeon would admire. Rarely must a weasel strike twice, even when its prey are large rabbits or squirrels, rather than its more customary fare of smaller mice, birds, insects, shrews, snakes and frogs.

Once a weasel has picked up a scent, the conclusion is virtually inevitable. There are few animals that can escape its detection or pursuit, for its body is so slim and its legs so short and adaptive that it can pursue a tiny mouse to the end of its burrow or a snake to its den deep within a seemingly impenetrable stone wall.

The weasel is one of the few woodland residents that is deservedly considered bloodthirsty, not only because it relishes blood — and brain tissue — but because it kills without what we would call "justification." Even a full-bellied weasel cannot pass a fresh scent without investigating . . . and that means almost certain death to whatever left the scent.

The animal's bloodthirsty nature and low-slung stature mean it can become something of a pest, squeezing through knotholes and cracks to reach such domestic shed and coop residents as ducks and chickens, dining on both the birds and their eggs. Such raids occasionally are carried out with no intention of eating and the intruder will simply litter the premises with the often decapitated remains of its victims. These devastations are fortunately rare and more than compensated for by the weasel's almost daily reduction or containment of mice, rats and other agriculturally nettlesome creatures. Without the weasel, the hawk and the owl, farmers and fowl-raisers would find themselves in far more dire straits than inflation and taxes can cause.

The weasel is an utterly fearless animal, one that will attack humans if sufficiently provoked. I have had staring contests with a few, always bowing to their silent, icy glare that means nothing less than "get out of my territory."

There are reasonably well documented reports of weasels attacking cattle, but I assume such incidents are the result of tick infestation of the cattle and the consequent presence of blood on their shoulders and flanks. Can you imagine a 10-ounce weasel trying to fell an adult steer?

A weasel will follow its prey almost anywhere, leaping into trees and water, although it is neither as adept a climber as a squirrel nor as accomplished a swimmer as a frog. Very few small, exclusively terrestrial animals have a chance of escaping a weasel once they have actually been spotted and while it is pure myth that weasels (and other animals) can hypnotize their prey, there are indications that some victims become so frightened that they cannot move. I, too, would be terrified into immobility were I to come face-to-face with a six-foot weasel. Thankfully, there are no such beasts abroad on the back forty, or anywhere else that I know of.

The weasel is known by a variety of other names, among them "polecat" and "ermine," and some of these titles apply to particular varieties of the animal. The least weasel, measuring up to eight inches in length (including its tail) and seldom weighing more than two ounces, is one of the world's smallest carnivores. The larger short- and long-tailed weasels measure up to 13 and 18 inches and weigh up to 5 and 12 ounces, respectively.

Weasels are typically brown in color, though it is not unusual to find individuals or groups with shades of black, red and yellow. Some are bridled with pale yellow and the great naturalist John James Audubon thought them to be entirely different creatures. Within the northernmost areas of their range, weasels turn entirely white during the winter months — with the notable exception of the black tips of their tails — and are then known as "ermine," highly valued and exhaustively trapped for their pelts.

Sometimes assuming ownership of its prey's burrow or den, the weasel is not what you would call a "tidy" animal, dragging chunks of its meals home and shoving them into convenient crevices where they often rot without being touched again. While most naturalists contend that the weasel is a virtually constant hunter because of its appetite and demeanor, I would submit that anything that lives in such foul quarters can be expected to do most anything.

The weasel is additionally foul in that it is a relative of the skunk and is blessed with the same pair of musk glands with which to dissuade its few natural enemies. Some woodsmen claim the weasel's glandular stench is more repelling than that of the skunk. I find that rather hard to believe, but I certainly am not about to purposefully find out.

On broad and silent wings they come, shrouded in darkness, honored and revered for thousands upon thousands of years by awed and fearful peoples.

They are the owls, symbols of wisdom, death and night.

Very few people will ever see an owl in the wild — though most who have spent a few hours in the woods have almost certainly been seen BY an owl — and only slightly more will hear its haunting call. That is unfortunate, for the owl is a creature of astonishing, almost unbelievable qualities.

The owl is also a sensationalized bird. Newspapers and radio and television stations throughout the land carefully document the cyclical winter appearance of snowy owls but seldom reserve an inch or a moment for more exceptional avian events. Perhaps we yet revere the bird, heeding a subconscious echo from awed ancestors long changed from flesh to dust.

One can easily understand the curiosity humans show for the owl, but how we came to consider it wise is another matter. Several other birds, including crows, are significantly more intelligent than owls, but owls *appear* smarter. It is a subtle thing. The eyes of owls face directly forward, unlike those of other birds. Relatively few other animals — primates and other birds of prey, for example — are so equipped with what is known as "binocular vision," the ability to focus on an object with both eyes. Humans, of course, have such ocular talents and are rather intelligent animals. That is the equation: if A is smart and B looks like A, then B must also be smart.

The owl is not dumb, mind you, but it is hardly as smart as we think.

Neither is the owl a strictly nocturnal bird. Though the majority spend their days in silent, secretive rest, all *can* see during the daylight hours and some, such as the breathtaking snowy, normally live so far to the "nightless" north that they care not what time of day they hunt. Many an owl-hating crow has discovered too late that an apparently lethargic, day-roosting snowy is far from defenseless.

Unlike humans, owls have eyes that are stationary. Whereas we can rotate our eyeballs to see objects to either side of us without moving our heads, the owl cannot. Instead, it has the ability to turn its head 180 degrees in either direction.

Barred Owl   John Patriquin

All owls have "facial discs" or concave arrangements of feathers radiating from the eyes in roughly circular patterns, though in some owls the discs are insignificant. The discs not only assist the bird's incredible powers of sight but serve as sound traps, directing sound toward its large ear openings. The owl's visual powers are justly famous, but its hearing is perhaps even more refined. Laboratory tests have proven that the birds can capture prey in total darkness. Cats and other famous night hunters, on the other hand, must rely to varying degrees on sight, expanding their pupils to utilize the often miniscule quantities of available light always present in night-draped woods, fields and barrens.

The owl's hunting talents are further enhanced by virtually noiseless flight. Its wings are large compared to its body and its flight feathers have a velvety surface that muffles the sound of passing air. Few of an owl's victims ever know the fate that has befallen them.

Although owls are fairly secretive birds, their presence is fairly easy to detect. Not only do they vocalize frequently and often with considerable gusto, but they regurgitate the bones, fur, beaks and other indigestible parts of their prey beneath their roosts, sometimes creating a heap of brown-gray pellets several inches deep. Researchers have long recognized the pellets as accurate catalogues of owls' preferred foods, though the task of poking through the pellets and identifying their contents is hardly exciting and very monotonous.

The study of owl pellets tends to support the contention that the birds are not consistent threats to such barnyard animals as chickens, though one can hardly expect them to ignore anything that is easy prey. On the other hand, owls relish the vermin that take such a toll on backyard animals and their young.

But all the facts and figures of the owl seem unimportant when darkness falls and its haunting call tumbles across the woods and fields. It is a sound of primeval tenor, mysterious in its disembodiment and symbolic of all that is wild.

Owls are wise, oxen dumb and snakes evil. It is curious how easily and unquestioningly we attach essentially human qualities to other animals, but in some instances such associations are entirely fitting.

The fox is indeed a sly and cunning rascal, capable of outwitting most humans in a fashion and with an ease that can be downright humiliating. It is no coincidence that the fox is so highly valued as a sporting game animal on both sides of the Atlantic: people prefer to pit themselves against animals whose conquest means something. Very few folks brag about "the porcupine that got away."

I have seen only a handful of foxes on the back forty during my years as tenant-owner, not because their numbers are few but because they are exasperatingly elusive. Now and then, while retracing my steps along the ridge trail or logging road, I have found fox tracks superimposed on the imprints left by my boots a short time before, testimony to one of the animal's most cunning ploys.

The fox is no numbskull. It knows through generations of observing humans that we tend to stir up all manner of beasts during our generally noisy woodland forays, so it just pads along behind at a safe distance. Should the fox's "guide" stumble upon and stop to examine a bird's nest, for example, the fox will quickly take both notice and any birds or eggs that happen to be in the nest.

A fox will even follow an old human scent — and those left by domestic cats and dogs — because it appreciates the fact that we seem incapable of discovering an animal's dwelling without pausing to poke, prod, touch and otherwise call attention to its location. And because of our size and visual perspective, we are often able to find nests, dens and other animal dwellings which even the fox may miss.

People have varying opinions about foxes, ranging from complete dread to perilous affection.

Captured when very young, foxes make excellent (but illegal) pets ... for a time. As members of the canine family, they exhibit many of the admirable and endearing qualities of a house dog, but as naturally wild and self-sufficient creatures, they frequently become ill-tempered as they grow older. It is difficult to erase the firm imprint of wildness. Many a well-meaning fox keeper has been suddenly and severely bitten by what had been an apparently docile and affectionate "pet."

The subject of fox bites leads naturally and necessarily to the subject of rabies. Foxes are among the most common carriers of rabies and occasionally precipitate localized epidemics of the dreaded disease.

Eastern Pennsylvania experienced such an outbreak in 1952 when domestic animals and people alike were bitten by foxes so deranged by the malady that some even hurled themselves in front of moving cars. One obviously rabid fox pursued a dog into a farmhouse kitchen where three children were playing, but the animal was fortunately "brushed" away by the youngsters' broom-toting mother. Tests conducted in Georgia during the mid-1940s

Red Fox   Irene Vandermolen

Young Red Fox   Leonard Lee Rue III

indicated that fully one-third of the state's foxes were then infected.

Such epidemics are thankfully rare and seem to occur only when the animal's population outstrips its habitat and resources. Increased hunting pressure and systematic poisonings in overpopulated regions have apparently all but eliminated the possibility of future massive outbreaks.

Caution is nevertheless mandatory when dealing with foxes, wild or domesticated.

Foxes are additionally nettlesome animals because they have developed a pronounced taste for poultry. State agriculture officials in Maine blamed them for killing nearly 13,000 laying hens in 1937 alone. There is not much one can do to dissuade a fox once it has discovered a flock of domestic birds. Some people insist a tarred rope encircling a coop or pen along the ground deters them and others claim foxes so dislike sulphur and turpentine that either, spread directly on the ground or coop foundation, will at least make a marauder think twice about conducting a full-scale raid.

Like the weasel and the owl, the fox has its redeeming features, not the least of which is its regular diet of rats, mice and other farm pests. In some areas where rabbits, squirrels and other small mammals have become overpopulated, the fox has been systematically and successfully reintroduced as a control mechanism.

The fox common in the Northeast is the red fox, a 15-pounder that, despite its title, occurs in shades of gray, silver and black. In its gray phase, it sometimes is mistaken for a gray fox, a rarity in the region that is distinguished by its salt-and-pepper coat and a tail tipped with black rather than white.

The fox is an admirably adaptive animal, revamping woodchuck burrows and other cavities to suit its needs or, in rare cases, setting up housekeeping beneath chicken coops or barns. Blessed with an exceptional sense of smell and hearing and sufficient speed to keep pace with a frightened rabbit, it can hear a mouse squeaking at nearly 50 yards and hunt by either stealth or speed.

It is that very adaptiveness that has enabled the fox to survive the onslaught of civilization. It has, in fact, benefitted from the presence of humans, learning and utilizing our tricks and our shortcomings. Just ask the one behind you.

* * *

The glaciers are coming! The glaciers are coming! Maybe. Only our great-great-great-great-great-etc. grandchildren will know for sure, but the ice sheets have been this way before, leaving the landscape as an eloquent witness to their passing.

For several thousands of years, until about 25,000 years ago, a vast ocean of ice grated southward from central Canada, burying the northern reaches of what is today the United States and changing forever the character of the land it touched. Its signature is everywhere.

What may once have been awesomely precipitous mountains are now gentle rolling hills. Equally gentle valleys are punctuated by round or oval heaps of rock. The ground itself is littered with variously shattered, polished and scratched stone. New rivers wind from new lakes to old seas.

The changes were immense. They could not have been otherwise, considering the circumstances, just as you or I would not look quite the same if struck by a bulldozer.

Ridges of gravel left by the retreating ice provide superb road-building materials and are commonly referred to as "hog-backs" or "horse-backs." Even relatively small ridges of gravel qualify as glacial evidence, though many have been masked by erosion and vegetation. Moraines, heaps of variously shaped rocks, were also deposited by the ice and perhaps the most famous moraine of all is New York's Long Island. Obviously, moraines tend to be rather more sizeable than hog-backs, though some of the latter exceed

Glacier-Carved Landscape   Maine Development Commission; George French

100 miles in length.

The ice did not deposit all its debris in such an orderly, linear fashion, however, often dropping huge boulders in the centers of what are now otherwise very undistinguished fields. The back forty has one such boulder, a nearly perfect sphere with a diameter in excess of 15 feet. It lies on the northern flank of a small hog-back, a most singular reminder of the ice's capabilities.

Some inland areas of the New England coastal plain, most notably in the vicinity of Freeport and Leeds in Maine, contain significant deposits of very fine sand. These deposits were not left by any glacier, per se, but by an ocean whose volume grew in direct proportion to the melting retreat of the last ice sheet. These ribbons of sand, some of which are certainly still undetected, are prehistoric beaches.

Because the glaciers carried so much debris, they treated the land much as coarse sandpaper treats wood. Here and there, one can find bared stretches of bedrock criss-crossed with scratches left by the rock-carrying ice. Bedrock also sometimes contains "glacial mills," holes ground into the rock by stones which sank to the bottom of a glacier and were slowly rotated by water falling through the shaft produced by its sinking. On rare occasions, the "grinding stone" remains, reduced to a tiny pebble at the bottom of the mill. (Rivers and streams that run over bedrock also may contain such mills, created when stones become lodged in crevices or depressions and are slowly rotated by the passing water.)

While specific examples such as these serve to adequately indicate the incomparable power of the glacier, it takes a patient eye and fertile imagination to truly perceive and appreciate what happened here so very long ago.

Look carefully at the landscape. It has been rubbed smooth, flattened under immense pressure and weight. "Cleansed," some would say. Its valleys descend gently to meandering rivers which flow to bays dotted by islands that once were inland hills or clutches of rock within a glacier's womb.

New England has actually been visited by four major glaciers in the past three-plus million years, but the forces that led to the advance of the first ice sheet (and hence its predecessors) were set in motion more than 60 million years ago. By those standards, it was only yesterday that the most recent glacier receded. We are, in fact, still living in the so-called "Ice Age." The ponderous sheets of ice, sometimes 10,000 feet thick, have vanished from this neck of the woods, but they have only retreated to steep-walled havens in Greenland, Alaska and Antarctica. They may be back.

Maine Fish & Game Dept.

WINTER

Steve Bowler

SNOW & ICE

The scent and taste of winter suddenly is upon the back forty, rattling the dry leaves and skimming the ponds with early morning ice.

Only the tenacious leaves of scattered oaks remain to interrupt the dull wash of naked hardwoods and the green islands of pine, spruce and hemlock. Even the brilliance of the white birches pales against the drab background.

Rigid with frost, the grass and weeds crackle under foot, denying stealth to the morning walker who would commune with the furred and feathered.

The sky, too, has donned its winter mask, furrowed with chill clouds and raked by bitter winds. With subtle, veiled expression, it echoes the season.

The housecats, like the sky, speak wordlessly of change. They are restless now, dashing from room to room and crying at the mudroom door, confused and anxious. Their bodies inform them of the change, of the vanished and the coming, but understanding is beyond their grasp. Or is it?

Summer's birds have been thoroughly displaced by those of winter. The warbler has yielded to the sparrow, the swallow to the jay and the wren to the junco. Soon the winter hawk, the sharp-shinned, will lay its claim to the treetops above the birdfeeders, waiting patiently for its meals.

Down from the mountains and lakes, the crows are flocking noisily above the field. Like so many thugs looking for a rumble, they roam the valleys and ridges in search of victims to bully and property to vandalize.

The squirrels have moved from their scattered nests to the pine grove behind the farmhouse, reacquainting themselves with winter nests hidden within the slash piles and ledge or among the stacks of lumber and boxes in the barn. There were seven of them, reds and grays, at the feeders yesterday and there should be twice or even thrice that number by mid-winter, provided the hawk contents itself with birds.

Deep within the back forty are the deer, facing now the most perilous time of year. The hunters of autumn are followed by the snows of winter and the snows will be followed by the dogs and coyotes. Each peril claims its share of their numbers.

Amid the rotting leaves at the bottom of the ponds, the last of yesterday's beetles and tadpoles seek shelter in the thick ooze.

Most have already slipped into the limbo of hibernation, but always there are a few stubborn individuals who remain unconvinced until ice-in time.

It is time for the raccoons to renew their nightly assaults on the feeders and garage and to clamber up the kitchen window should they find no meal in either place, there to scratch at the glass and yowl their ire. One of these years, I definitely will maintain a log of how much birdseed and how many apples, carrots, stale bread loaves and other delicacies are bought or salvaged for them and the other winter marauders.

Maybe next winter.

Josh went mildly bananas at the sight of it. He propped his chin on the kitchen windowsill and stared excitedly across the whitening lawn toward the first phalanx of dark pines.

It is the season's first snowfall, a thin cloak that mutes and muffles the woods, bringing an abrupt end to the drab nakedness of late autumn.

As I watch Josh's innocent, wide-eyed response to the overnight transformation of the world, I suddenly realize how very differently we adults react to the same phenomenon. We regard the first snowfall not as a thing of beauty, but as an enemy's first probing skirmish. The ensuing months, we convince ourselves, will be devoted to a full-scale war with the elements.

Winter is indeed a harsh time, a time to rethink our driving and walking habits, a time when friends and family withdraw to their own hearths. It is a time of potential peril, of overburdened roofs and crumpled automobiles. But it is also a gentle time for those who see and treat it as something other than a deadly foe.

Winter is the time to introduce children to sleds, nuthatches, toboggans and grandma's mittens.

Now is the time to learn how the deer fared during the hunting season, following their deeply rutted trails across the ridge and into the thickets beyond. It is time to prepare my "apple bar," a length of pine limb upon whose rounded spikes I place apples and other fruits intended for the deer but devoured by squirrels, raccoons and others, too.

It is time to introduce the kids to poor man's maple sugar candy, maple syrup (of the unadultered variety) poured directly onto fresh snow. The hardened globules of syrup are among the sweetest, most marvelous treats in the world.

It is time to set aside a few dollars from each paycheck with which to purchase sunflower seeds, millet, suet and thistle seed

John Patriquin

for the ravenous birds.

A single robin — a young one, judging by its slightly mottled chest — remains on the back forty, descending each morning on a crabapple tree already stripped of its fruit by a pair of brazen raccoons. Does the bird expect the tree to blossom and fruit at any moment? Like Josh, it is young and mystified.

The back forty is becoming famous among the animal populace of the area. With each sunrise, the feeder-festooned backyard takes on the appearance and hubbub of a fast-food franchise parking lot. Tracks in the snow tell us that it hardly has been devoid of activity during the nighttime, either.

Soon it will be time to sharpen the bowsaw and search out the most perfect Christmas tree the woodlot has to offer, a task that arouses mixed feelings stirred by my distaste for felling living trees. The emotional tug-of-war ends when, the cutting done, I turn my steps toward the distant farmhouse, saw on one shoulder and tree on the other. The tree's needles prick exposed wrists and face. Pitch adheres tenaciously to clothing, skin and hair.

Like coping with winter itself, cutting a Christmas tree can be a tedious, dirty process. But it can also be a joyful task, one that makes both the holiday and the entire season a time of rekindled admiration for the beauty that is to be found in most any place at most any time.

He is bound to ask, so I am trying to prepare a reasonable answer.

Josh is no longer young enough to simply marvel at the snow this winter. He will want to know where it comes from, what it's made of and why it's white. Simple things like that.

"Well, son, snow comes from the sky, is made of frozen water and is white because it reflects light."

"Sure, dad, but . . . ."

Snow is indeed frozen water, but frozen water is not snow, so the definition is incomplete. Sleet, for example, is a byproduct of snow, formed when snowflakes are carried by vertical air currents through areas of especially cold rain which freezes about the flakes. The air currents hold the flakes aloft and within the area of cold rain long enough for the process to run its course. Particularly strong winds will keep the flakes airborne until hail is produced.

Snowflakes themselves are colonies of snow crystals which are, in turn, formed about single ice crystals. The ice crystals are pro-

Isabel Lewando

duced in the atmosphere when below-freezing temperatures enable water vapor to condense on the surfaces of tiny particles.

The whole process brings to mind the old "legbone-connected-to-the-hipbone" song: the snowflake is connected to the snow crystal which is connected to the ice crystal which is connected to the particle. Not especially melodic, but it will do.

While snow is a purely wintertime phenomenon in most temperate regions, it is widely thought that the bulk of the earth's rainfall originates in the higher, colder atmosphere as snow. Indeed, high-altitude cirrus clouds are comprised of ice crystals, the parents of snow crystals and the grandparents of snowflakes.

Temperature variations produce varied crystal configurations. Thin, six-sided "plate" crystals are formed at temperatures just below freezing while hollow, columnar crystals are formed at lower temperatures and hollow, prismatic crystals are formed at even lower temperatures. Although no one can prove for certain that the infinite number of snowflakes that have fallen during Earth's history did not include two of exactly the same configuration, the common assumption is that each is a genuine individual. It is breathtaking enough to consider that no two people who have ever lived were exactly alike, but the prospect that no two snowflakes have ever been the same is downright staggering.

Despite the obvious drawbacks of snow — clogged highways, overburdened power lines, cracking roofs and the like — it certainly does have its benefits, though they may be hard to appreciate in midwinter when it is dealt with on terms that have little to do with aesthetics or pure function.

Snow is one of nature's most proficient insulators, for example, protecting small plants from low temperatures and killing winds. Some people insist it does a better job keeping out drafts than hay or pine boughs when heaped against a house foundation, but it is seldom available to blunt the winds of October and April. I know that the back forty farmhouse indeed is warmer once the snow has buried its crevice-filled granite foundation.

Because snow is condensed and frozen water vapor, it is an invaluable source of water when the springtime melt begins. Countless New England streams, ponds, swamps and sinkholes which support an endless array of life rely entirely on melted snow (and rain, much of which begins as snow) for their existence.

And, of course, snow has its benefits if you have an affection for skiing, snowshoeing, sledding, snowmobiling or tobogganing.

"Did you get all that, Josh?"

"Yup, dad, but . . . what does 'melting' mean?"

* * *

Regardless of how much data our textbooks and journals contain, animal behavior remains one of the most puzzling and enthralling fields of study. One of the greatest puzzlements within that broad discipline is hibernation.

Now is the time of year to be particularly cautious in the completion of outdoor tasks, for the slightest displacement of a log or stone can spell doom for otherwise protected creatures within or beneath. Animals which hibernate are in delicate limbo between life and death, safe until spring unless their quarters are invaded or disrupted.

As primarily hairless creatures, humans should understand quite easily the accepted reasons for hibernation.

The heat generated by animals' bodies is lost more rapidly during cold weather than during warm, something we are cognizant of if we step outdoors in January without a jacket. Just as our clothing helps to retain body heat, so many animals are protected from excessive heat loss by seasonally thicker coats of fur. But for most animals a thicker carpet is not the answer. They must generate more heat and to do so they merely eat more.

That is a simple enough proposition unless food sources and caches are covered by snow or encased in ice. Food gathering becomes difficult and it is the exceptional animal that can actually increase its diet under such circumstances.

The only viable alternatives are migration and hibernation, both of which are thought to be physiological responses to a changing climate, although the former seems to be at least partially behavioral in nature as well. It is not known exactly what triggers the urge to hibernate — possibly a biochemical action in the adrenal glands, some say — but the results are certain. The animal's heartbeat, breathing, circulation and body temperature drop. Its rate of breathing may decrease by as much as 99 percent and its body temperature to near freezing, though an as yet unknown mechanism arouses most whose temperatures dip dangerously low.

Most hibernators glut themselves before hibernation actually begins. Their lowered metabolism during hibernation means their stuffed bellies take longer to empty but, even when empty, a hibernator can usually resort to a "reserve tank" of nutrition in its body fats. The body weights of some hibernators may drop by 30 or 40 percent before spring, which partially explains the grouchy demeanor of some animals at that time of the year.

Despite the depth of "sleep" attained by some animals, woodland hikers who stumble upon them should not assume they are safe. A bear, for instance, can awaken quickly and without appreciable detriment to its keen senses.

Few of the larger warm-blooded animals are true hibernators, a distinction reserved for their smaller relatives such as brown bats and ground squirrels whose body temperatures drop to approximately that of the air in their nests or dens.

Even the smaller warm-blooded animals can nonetheless awaken quickly and at almost any time, regardless of the fact that they are considered the champion sleepers of the animal realm.

The real champions are the cold-blooded animals. Frogs, salamanders, lizards, snakes and some fish bury themselves in soft earth, mud or sand to hibernate, below the depths normally reached by ground frost. Their body temperatures drop so sharply that they seem dead. Those caught above the frost line often are.

Insects, including the larval stages of some moths and butterflies, seek out crevices in rocks and tree bark, the latter refuges being well known to woodpeckers, nuthatches and chickadees who consume a significant portion of the hapless sleepers.

Some animals, most notably the bats, "hibernate" on a daily basis throughout the year, their body temperatures falling to that of the air about them whenever they sleep. Because their "hibernation" is so brief and regular, naturalists refer to it as "torpidity" rather than true hibernation.

Hibernation is by no means limited to the animals of the world's colder regions: some which inhabit especially dry and hot regions seek shelter during periods of excessive drought and attain a state of hibernation referred to as "estivation."

Hibernating animals have always faced grave dangers from non-hibernating predators and the weather, but humans have provided some new and equally threatening perils. House cats and renegade dogs represent serious threats to those hibernators which awaken and venture forth periodically. Their mobility and, in some cases, senses decreased by sleep and cold, these briefly awakened hibernators are easy prey.

Snowmobiles and other mechanized intruders pose another kind of threat altogether, one which has nothing to do with their operators' behavior and attitudes. These machines compact the snow, especially in suburban fields where they are used to excess, creating a layer of hard-packed snow or ice at ground level and trapping hibernating rodents in their dens. Unable to reach adjoining, above-ground caches or food, the animals starve or resort to cannibalism.

There is little we can do to blunt these perils, but we certainly can continue to marvel at the mystery beneath the snow.

* * *

Black ice! I had thought the two back forty ponds were too sullied to freeze "black," but they have.

Pressing my face against the ice, I can see the leaves, pine needles and other debris cloaking the bottom less than a yard below. Only a handful of small bubbles and some thin cracks intrude; otherwise the view is clear and clean, a four-inch thick window to a world seldom seen.

It brings to mind winter days long ago, of hours gliding across a black Sewell Pond in Arrowsic, of my mother executing graceful leaps and loops on a Christmas Cove ice pond. I recall, too, my Uncle George and our afternoon jaunts up the Concord River in

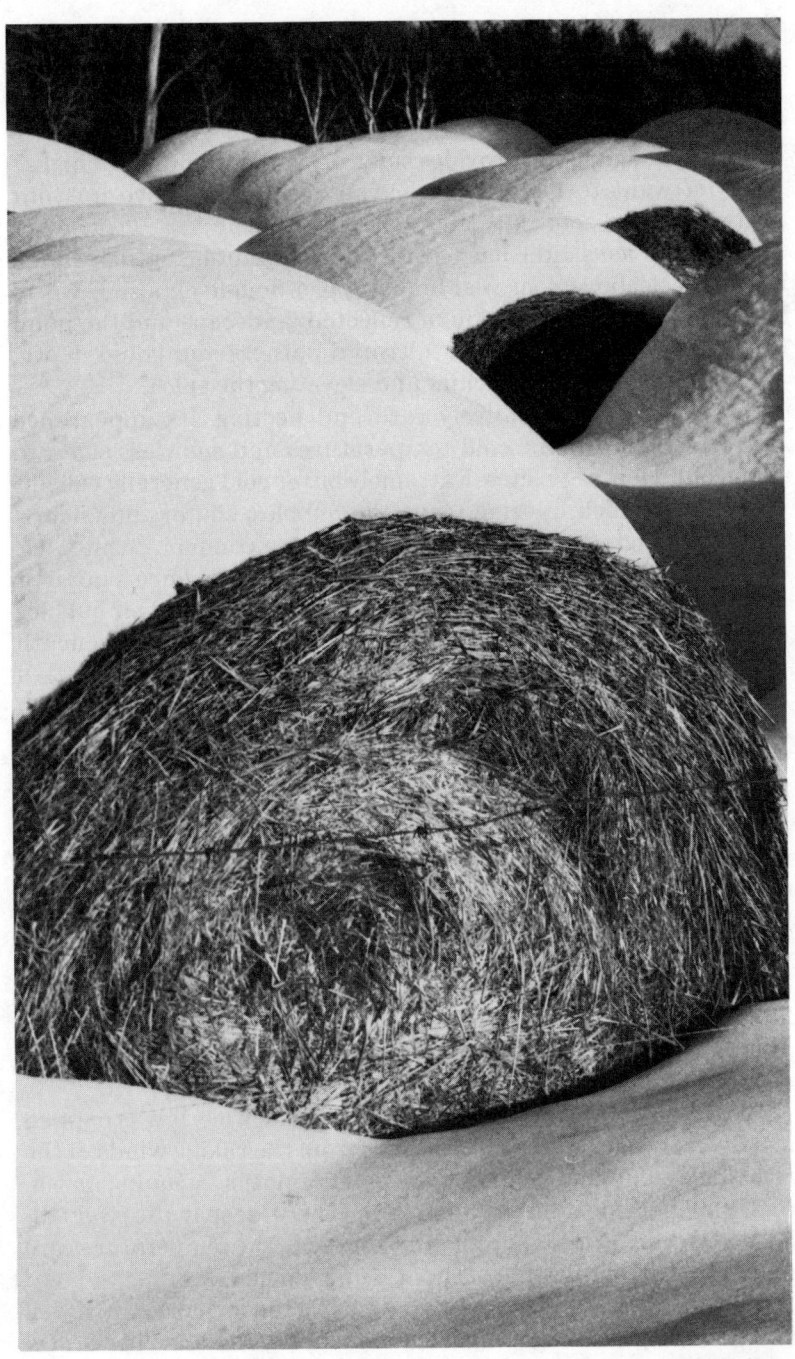

Merry Farnum

Massachusetts, from the "rude bridge" nearly to Bedford.

Black ice skating is like no other skating. There are some who insist there is nothing like it, period, though I assume they are ignoring some indoor sports that I will not discuss here. I also suspect that hang-gliding provides some of the same euphoric "highs."

If you want to fly without leaving the ground, lace up your skates and find some black ice.

The black ice skater has the distinct sense of being suspended several feet above a surreal landscape, a double-exposure world formed by the juxtaposition of reflected landscape and the pond bottom. It is a landscape of mirrored flatness and liquid depth, confounding one's equilibrium and elevating the spirit.

But black ice is relatively rare and fleeting. Its appearance hinges on calm winds, cold temperatures and snowless skies, to name but a few requisites. Extremely bitter cold generally will not do because quick freezing traps the bubbles, silt, organic debris and other ingredients that create the more common "white" ice. Black ice is normally a brief phenomenon because once a pond or lake has been covered by a sheen of ice, the debris and air bubbles constantly rising from its depths become trapped just beneath the initial layer, clouding subsequent ice formation. Snow, too, is a threat to black ice. Not only does it hide the ice itself, but wind-driven snow, especially of the granular variety, can "sandpaper" the ice-covered surface of a pond or lake until its transparency is destroyed.

There are exceptions, of course. Returning from northern Maine in a raging snowstorm one week, a friend and I came upon a Kennebec River backwater with not one, but three distinct layers of black ice. Looking down upon the five-acre backwater from a bordering ridge, we could count the layers by their successive, crisscrossing fractures. Judging by the depth of the fractures, each layer was about six inches thick. The entire backwater looked much like a piece of fine, though randomly constructed, lace, delicate but imposing in the strength of its craftsmanship.

The backwater had all the requisites for black ice. It was cupped in a deep bowl, protected on all sides from the raking winds of the river valley, and had no detectable inlet or outlet, meaning its waters remained constantly tranquil. And there, deep in the river valley and ringed by its own rock-and-dirt wall, the temperatures are no doubt sufficiently chill without being "quick."

But the snows are coming again and, like the memories of Sewell Pond and Uncle George, this season's black ice soon will be a new addition to my mental scrapbook.

171

Guy Gannett Publishing Co.

Black-Capped Chickadee   Leonard Lee Rue III

SNOW BIRDS

Operating a winter feeding station for winterbound birds is one thing. Feeding them by hand is another matter, an achievement that is well worth the time and effort to realize.

I became interested in hand feeding wild birds several years ago and purely by chance. It was an early January morning, I recall, when I stepped from the garage to refill our clutch of feeders in the backyard. No sooner had I closed the door behind me than I was literally inundated by a flock of some 40 redpolls, pinkish wads of energy slightly smaller than a chickadee.

After regaining my composure, such as it is at dawn, I trudged to the feeders with my bags of sunflower, thistle and millet seed, carrying at least a half-dozen redpolls on my cap and shoulders. Residents of the deep northern woods, these birds seldom encounter humans and hence are exceptionally trusting. This particular flock proved simply unnerving, setting up a great, twittering din that said just one thing: "Give us breakfast!"

I dutifully followed orders — for the next two months — and before the winter had ended most every bird utilizing the feeders had adopted the habits of the redpolls, alighting on my head and shoulders as soon as I appeared with my bags of seed. That was easy. The redpolls did all the work, convincing their squeamish cousins that I meant no harm and that they could therefore use my body as a table. The same results can be achieved with a healthy dose of patience.

The first step in a hand-feeding endeavor is to establish a feeding station in the early fall, permitting the birds to enjoy its fare without human intrusion until the ground is snow-covered for the season. Once they have become settled, make it a practice to remain near the feeders for several minutes whenever you fill them. Thirty or 40 feet is a good distance to start with.

After three or four days at that distance, move to within 10 or 15 feet of the feeders, standing absolutely still for several minutes at each visit.

Two or three days later, move still closer, but at this point it is wise to select a single sunflower seed feeder as your "target." Sunflower seeds are the favorite fare of chickadees and they are normally the easiest to hand feed. Spend as many days as seems practical standing a mere three or four feet from the target feeder. If the birds seem undisturbed, coming to the feeder during your presence, it is time for the final step.

Tree Sparrow   Leonard Lee Rue III

Male Goldfinch in Winter Garb   Leonard Lee Rue III

When the birds seem to have accepted you as something akin to a tree or other harmless object, permit the feeders to empty during the day, though not so much so that the birds have no evening meal. Make your morning visit to the feeders the following day, but do not fill them: resume your position three or four feet from the feeder and extend one hand toward the feeder, a dozen or so sunflower seeds cradled in the upturned, open palm.

The birds' "moment of decision" has arrived. They will or will not come to your hand. Be patient, for it may take several minutes for the first to make up its mind. Chickadees, especially, will flutter inches from an extended hand several times before alighting. If there are no "takers" after 10 minutes or so, refill the feeders and repeat the procedure the following morning. It will work, sooner or later.

The principal rule in hand feeding any wild bird is to remain absolutely motionless. Even an innocent swallow to clear your throat can send birds diving into the nearest thicket in utter terror: many a predator precedes its final lunge with a gulp, clearing its throat for the morsel awaiting. A blink of an eye can be similarly upsetting.

It often is helpful to wear the same clothes when hand feeding wild birds, or at least the same jacket and hat. Birds are not very accomplished in the art of facial recognition, but they can tell a puffy parka from a dungaree jacket and a tasseled cap from a bowler.

Never, *never* close your hand about a bird. Its presence on your hand is evidence that it has come to trust you: do not destroy that gift. The only exception to this rule is one which I have never been in a position to exercise. If a bird has a thin aluminum band about one leg, the bird can be gently held long enough to read the band and forward its number to the appropriate research authorities.

If family members or friends wish to try feeding your winter flocks by hand, let them, but establish the ground rules and see that they are followed. Some wintering flocks are more trusting than others and will readily accept seed from strangers, but that is very much the exception and has much to do with the proximity of such distracting influences as highways and other houses.

Once your birds have accepted seed from your hand, they probably will continue to do so for the remainder of the winter, regardless of the feeder supply. By no means should you stop filling your feeders: unless you hand feed your birds throughout the day they cannot possibly survive solely from the hand. And there are many species that simply refuse to be fed from a human hand.

Chickadees are the easiest of New England's wintering birds to hand feed, with the exception of such northern rarities as the redpoll. Nuthatches usually wait for the chickadees to make up their minds before eating from a hand. Goldfinches, pine siskins, some sparrows and blue jays will also eat from a hand, though the jays are often too nervous to do so consistently.

It is a time-consuming process. A successful hand feeding endeavor is indescribably rewarding, however, and gives the cold winter months an added dimension of color and companionship.

She first appeared two weeks ago, sticking her head nervously around the woodpile between pecks at the cracked corn and millet beneath the nearby birdfeeder.

The back forty is not ideal pheasant country, but the birds do visit now and then. This particular hen has apparently decided to stay, drawn by an abundance of food she cannot hope to find in the snow-covered woods and fields.

She comes each morning at about 9 o'clock and often visits

Ring-necked Pheasant   Maine Fish & Game Dept.

again just before dusk, following her kind's typical feeding schedule. She seems to prefer the company of the 30-odd mourning doves to that of other birds, though I suspect she would welcome the arrival of another pheasant.

Her nights are spent somewhere in the vicinity of the larger pond nearly 100 yards from her favorite feeder, so she is hardly exhausting herself on the way to and from the dining table. She is a smart one.

Pheasants are not known for their intelligence. They are not dumb, mind you, but their circumstances and habits produce the impression of stupidity. They run around in cities. They congregate in the open. They frequently prefer to remain motionless while hunters take careful aim. In other words, they act dumb, but in this case dumbness is in the mind of the beholder. Pheasants quite simply are not a natural part of our scenery and, therefore, do not act as we may expect them to.

The common ring-necked pheasant of our fields and open woodlands is a native of Asia. The first successful introduction of the bird to this continent came in 1880-1881 when O. N. Denny, then the American consul-general to Shanghai, China, shipped 22 cocks and 20 hens to the Willamette Valley of Oregon. Earlier attempts, including one in 1790 by the governor of New Hampshire, had failed miserably, but Denny's attempt was a resounding success. By 1892 the Oregon birds were so numerous that a 10-week hunting season was declared and it is commonly reported that 50,000 birds were shot on the very first day.

The success of Denny's experiment prompted other individuals and states to try again and in 1899 shipments of breeding stock were recorded to more than 500 localities from Alaska to Mexico.

The ring-necked now flourishes in most every state, except in the deep South. "Flourishes" is perhaps a bad term to use, for the bird does not have an easy time of it in the northern tier of states.

Pheasants are primarily terrestrial birds. They feed and nest on the ground and even prefer to walk away from danger rather than to take wing, although they are strong and rapid flyers. When they do fly, however, they rise quickly into the air and then drop back to the ground a relatively short distance away, much as grouse are prone to do.

Northern pheasants suffer greatly during harsh winters when their customary fare of weed seeds, dried berries and the like is covered. Under such conditions, they rely on backyard feeders and barnyard leftovers for their survival. They become less and less wary, often even tame, and when the next hunting season rolls around are likely to be "sitting ducks."

That is what worries me about this particular bird. If it has decided to stick around for the duration of the winter, chances are good that it will not appear during the next one. But we are not going to turn it away. Neither will we make any overt attempt to tame her. We will just wait and see.

The hawk's wings fanned across the crusty snow and its head turned quickly from side to side as it pressed the screaming blue jay into the snow.

Nearly as large as its captor, the blue jay struggled to escape. The hawk held the jay's neck firmly in one talon, preventing its strong beak from reaching its vulnerable eyes. Within moments of the swift and silent attack, the jay had summoned its companions from throughout the nearby woodlands. One by one, they plummeted from the trees ringing the backyard, screaming their anger at the hawk as they flashed past its outspread form.

The hawk was a sharp-shinned, a smallish bird as hawks go and distinguishable from the Cooper's hawk only by its slightly squared-off tail: the Cooper's tail is slightly rounded and although it is also a slightly larger bird than the sharp-shinned, the differences in size are usually beyond detection in the field.

This sharp-shinned was an immature bird, brown where its elders are blue-gray and red-brown. Perhaps it was that immaturity which prompted the attack on such a large bird as the jay. While sharp-shinned hawks can easily lift a jay from the ground, this particular individual seemed unable to do so. It would have had a considerably easier time of it had a chickadee been selected instead of the jay.

The sight of a hawk on its prey may seem gruesome, even brutal, to the uninitiated, but to those who understand and appreciate the intricacies of the bird world it is a sight to be savored. Interference is taboo.

I interfered. Opening the door from the borning room to the yard, I frightened the hawk from its intended meal with a flailing of my arms. The jay promptly flew away with a chorus of shrieks and a cloud of small feathers.

I should not have interfered, though I reasoned that the jay was likely to die slowly and with considerable agony whereas a chickadee or sparrow would have died on impact. Regardless of those considerations, I should not have driven the hawk from the jay. Perhaps the victim's dozen or so friends would have achieved the same result: their rather clumsy dives and raucous cries were

Red-tailed Hawk   Fred Tilly

obviously bothering the hawk. Maybe the hawk would have abandoned its prey: it was making no attempt to deliver the final, killing blow and appeared wary of dining in the open where it had trapped the bird.

The hawk will no doubt return. Its attack on the jay marked the third consecutive winter that a sharp-shinned has appeared at our feeders and in each case the bird has stayed throughout the winter, regularly snatching birds from the ground or feeders.

The winter hawk is an especially secretive and resourceful bird, whispering through the bare trees or sitting without motion in an evergreen grove. It is a bird, this multi-specied winter hawk, whose instincts and strength are put to the ultimate test.

Most hawks which frequent the back forty in wintertime are northern birds, pressed southward by dwindling food supplies and deepening snow. The deeper the snow and the scarcer their food, the greater their numbers here. Neither the sharp-shinned nor the Cooper's are purely northern birds, inhabiting much of the United States, but their numbers increase markedly during the winter months and although reclusive in nature they necessarily draw ever closer to houses and their feeding stations.

There is little that can or should be done when a hawk decides to frequent a feeding station. They can be frightened away with ease, but they invariably return, striking quickly and with breathtaking accuracy. A sparrow "rescued" from a hawk is seldom truly rescued, even if it appears healthy, for the trauma of the attack will soon take its toll and the bird will probably die, wracked by tremors and fear.

A hawk knows a good thing when it sees it and tops on its "good things" list is the feeding station, a cornucopia of meat that cannot go unravished. It was not so very long ago that people routinely shot or trapped hawks that developed a taste for feeder or barnyard birds. But scientific research has demonstrated beyond a doubt that such wanton slaughter is both pointless and self-defeating.

The hawk is one of the most insatiable eaters of mice, rats and other rodents that carry disease to poultry pens and which decimate the natural seed crop so valuable to both wild and domestic birds. Moreover, rodents have a proven appetite for birds themselves, particularly for the young. Without some means of checking the rodent population, domestic and wild birds are subjected to incredible slaughter. Hawks are a most natural and effective check: without them we would be forced to resort to pesticides and traps, neither of which can discriminate between rodents and barnyard or house animals.

It is an act steeped in ignorance to kill a hawk, an act prompted by the application of human standards to animals whose "standards" are determined by instinct and pure necessity. Hawks will dine somewhere, whether within or beyond human sight, and we have no right or reason to call the act brutal. It is, however, understandable for a bird-loving human to feel anger or frustration at the sight of a hawk disappearing into the woods with a sparrow held tightly in its talons.

Such is a fairly common sight at this time of year, however, as hawks follow their prey to feeding stations. Their attacks are consequently more obvious and, it seems, more merciless. But mercy is largely a human virtue which we must not routinely expect of other animals. A hawk without mercy is one whose prey dies quickly and anyone who is bothered by the sight of a slow-dying bird or mouse should applaud the absence of mercy in the hawk's breast.

Marvel, if you will, at the winter hawk.

Watch as it climbs the frosty air or plummets silently from a treetop, wingtips gripping the air and talons spread wide with anxious hunger. The hawk is a bird to be admired and it is now, during the winter months, that we have the opportunity to nurture that admiration.

The tufted titmouse did it!

I did not realize it at the time, but when one of the little Southerners showed up at our feeders last week it represented the 100th kind of bird to visit the back forty since I began keeping track of such things a few years ago. I have every hope of reaching the 125-bird watermark within the next two or three years.

Now, all this fuss about a few score birds may not seem like a big deal to many people, but there is a point to it.

More than a few die-hard birders will go to most any extreme to add a rarity to their "life lists," rosters of lifetime sightings maintained by most birdwatchers. Some will travel to the opposite side of the planet to add an obscure sparrow to their list and a growing number of tour operators cater specifically to that breed, ferrying them to mid-ocean in search of albatrosses or to a particular Michigan county to track down the elusive Kirtland's warbler.

There are even a handful of obviously wealthy birdwatchers who do little else with their time but seek out rarities and their life lists are longer even than the line in a doctor's waiting room. They are the fanatics of the birding community, bird "nuts" with the money and the time to follow feathers wherever they are to be found.

Birdwatchers as a whole are the subject of outlandish caricature that borders on ridicule, portrayed as elderly, stiff-limbed folks garbed entirely and constantly in tweed and festooned with binoculars, field guides and cameras. While that image may occasionally be accurate, it is all too readily applied to all birdwatchers and tends to belittle their admirable devotion and scientific contributions.

Maintaining geographical or life lists of bird sightings can be no more than self-effacing statements of real or imagined expertise or vehicles of greater environmental understanding and sensitivity. One who catalogues the birds or other natural residents of his or her surroundings is one who is more aware of the delicate interrelationships involved. And awareness is the keystone of proper management and protection.

Birders who keep records of the residents of and visitors to their back forties and backyards are likely to understand the consequences of change therein. They know, for example, that the loss of a certain kind of tree is apt to mean the loss of birds that require or prefer those trees for nesting or feeding. The enlargement of a pond will probably encourage visits by larger ducks or the nesting of ducks that previously only visited during their migrations.

On a national — indeed international — scale, birdwatchers contribute to massive rosters of wintering, nesting and migrating birds that ultimately give researchers a clear picture of population levels and trends. National environmental policies often hinge on such data: if a certain wood warbler of limited breeding range is proven to be decreasing in numbers, that range might be legislatively protected in some fashion against development or commercial use.

Combined with meticulous banding programs, this sighting data, originating as a birdwatcher's list, also helps determine migration patterns and timetables, the knowledge of which is vital to the greater understanding of our world and its behavior and origins. Animal behavior, after all, is dictated by heredity and environment.

So, the next time you run across a birdwatcher, keep those facts in mind. You are not necessarily looking at an idle, nonproductive member of the leisure set. You are looking at an important cog in the eternal search for the key to what makes our world and its passengers tick.

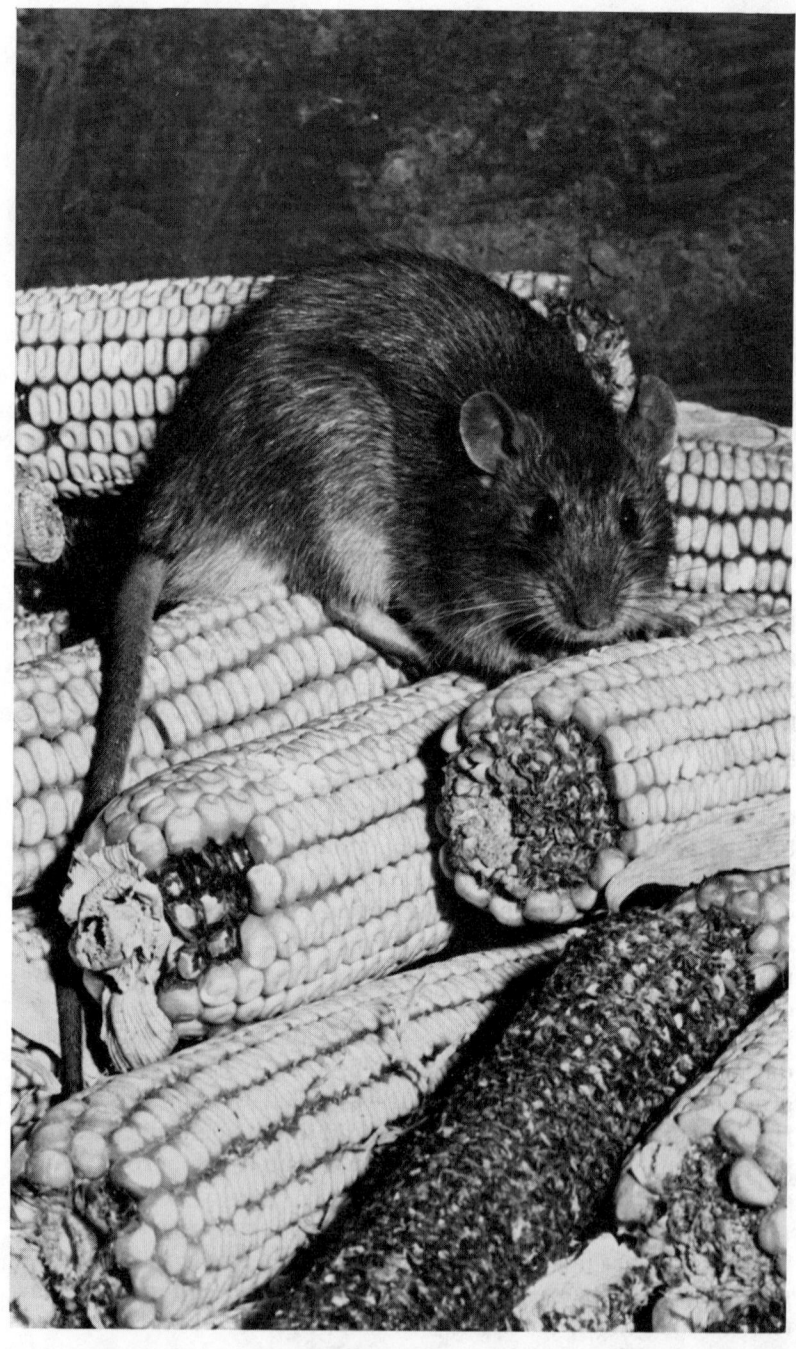

Norway Rat   Leonard Lee Rue III

SNOW BEASTS

Rat.

Mere mention of the beast is enough to scare the suspenders off most folks. What is more, those fears are justified, if somewhat overdone.

It is true, for example, that the rat is the greatest carrier of disease that humankind has ever known, diseases that have killed more humans than anything else, including warfare. It is also true that rats have attacked and eaten humans, generally untended infants.

The rat is certainly not a loveable creature, but it is nonetheless an integral link in the chain of life. We have only ourselves to blame for its excessive numbers: its population and tenacity increase in direct proportion to our uncanny ability to produce filth.

Just as the unfortunate snake has become the symbol of human moral decay, so the rat has become the uncontested symbol of our society's physical decay. The snake's status is utterly undeserved while that of the rat ... well, the shoe fits.

Rats are among the most prolific land animals, bearing as many as 50 or even 60 young each year. When you stop to consider the fact that the young are sexually mature in about eight months, the full weight of the animal's impact on society becomes quite clear.

Besides carrying an array of diseases, including bubonic plague, rats are notorious destroyers of crops and poultry. It is estimated that they are responsible for some $200 million in property damage in this country each year.

Contrary to popular belief, rats are not pure urbanites. The brown and black rats of the East, which have a variety of local names, are common woodland residents and their numbers seldom approach those of their urban cousins because of the natural checks and balances of their habitats. They are especially common on active farms but can be found virtually anywhere, even in the remotest of forests.

One very rotund individual is spending this winter in a network of snow tunnels beneath the backyard birdfeeders, venturing forth now and then to snatch a mouthful of seed. It is not the only rat I have spotted on the back forty, but I understand they once were as common as pine needles. A young man who worked at the farm when it was still an active affair told me a while ago that the grain chutes in the barn sometimes contained more rats than kernels of corn. When the chutes were opened, he said, the rats would literally pour onto the floor in a great heap of chattering anger!

No matter how vile and dangerous rats may be, they have their niche in the world. They are adept scavengers, removing sources of perhaps as many diseases as they themselves carry. In some parts of this country they have become the principal food of other predators. And where would scientific research be without the lowly rat?

The rat's bad points far outweigh its good points, though, and they must be dealt with accordingly. Poisons and traps are the most common tools for waging war on rats, the former for large concentrations, the latter for less threatening numbers. It goes without saying that poisons — the most common being arsenic, strychnine, barium chloride and red squill — should be used with the utmost caution, if at all. The newer red squill is said to be harmless to humans and domestic animals, but what of the skunks, chipmunks, raccoons and squirrels that share our woods and lawns with the rat?

Unless you are dealing with a huge population of rats, perhaps the most logical and safest weapon is the trap, either the live trap that enables transportation of the animal to another location or spring traps that kill. Whatever trap is used, it should be thoroughly cleansed before and after use because rats can smell the slightest trace of both humans and deceased members of their own kind.

Chicken coops, sheds and barns can be ratproofed to a certain, though never quite adequate degree by covering their lower portions with narrow-mesh wire and filling holes in their foundations with concrete. But rats are persistent and are sufficiently adept climbers to make Spider Man look like a snail.

All refuse should be contained in heavy metal barrels — rats can chew through lead, however, though no one is likely to have a garbage can made of that metal — and discarded promptly. That is where I am faced with a dilemma: I provide table scraps for such visitors as raccoons and deer, but in so doing I am no doubt encouraging the rats. I have not decided what to do. After all, I like rats, too. In reasonable quantity.

What has four legs, beady eyes, whiskers and eats such things as Polish sausage, oranges and sunflower seeds?

Procyon lotor, that's who. The common raccoon, a cunning beast if ever there was one. Slyer than a fox. Dexterous as a monkey. Able to climb tall trees in a very brief minute.

Raccoon   Leonard Lee Rue III

A couple of 20-pounders have been robbing our birdfeeders for several weeks now, hunching across the backyard under cover of darkness to conduct their thievery. They know, too, that there is plenty of food inside the house and when they cannot find enough at the feeders they come to the doors and windows to stare longingly at the refrigerator and converse in low, throaty voices with the cats.

They are exasperatingly inventive and persistent. They had been robbing our suet feeder for more than a week before I decided to take remedial action, attaching the feeder to a clothesline with twisted and knotted picture frame wire. They simply clambered to the feeder across the clothesline, untwisted and unknotted the wire and spirited the thing away. I haven't seen it since.

That is why I have taken to tossing table scraps, including Polish sausage and oranges, onto the lawn: they seem to prefer such morsels to birdseed and so long as there is some around will leave the feeders pretty much alone. But in providing such fodder, I am telling them to be fruitful and multiply. I must wean them of our generosity when the snow begins to retreat.

Raccoons are cute. That is how children see them and they are quite right. But they can also be very, very mean. They are well equipped to take care of themselves in the woods, armed with razor-sharp teeth and deceptively strong and slashing claws. There are few predators, save the very hungry and very dumb, who dare challenge a healthy, full-grown raccoon.

If captured when very young, raccoons will become gentle pets, but they tend to develop a nasty streak toward the end of their 8- to 12-year lifespans and can show flashes of that character at any time. It is for that reason, and out of respect for the animal, that they should never be intentionally kept from their natural place in the wild.

Raccoons are prodigious eaters. They will tackle most anything, though their favorite dishes include frogs, berries, turtles, crayfish, fruit, nuts and young birds (including, unfortunately, barnyard fowl). They are appropriately well known for their habit of washing their food before eating: the *lotor* half of their Latin title means "a washer." But they are not so hygenic that they will carry their food any great distance just to wash it. If water is handy, they will dunk it, swish it and flail it about, sometimes for a considerable length of time.

Related to the far larger panda of Asia, the raccoon attains a length of nearly three feet from the tip of its nose to the tip of its bushy tail and may weigh as much as 30 pounds. It makes its home in hollow trees or rocky hillsides, excavating a den where an average of four blind and completely helpless young are born in March or April. The very young have a cry similar to that of a human baby, a sound that can be most unnerving to humans afoot in the night woods. They remain with their parents for as long as a year, foraging in small groups of black-masked bandits whose family squabbles can awaken the soundest of human sleepers.

While raccoons are adept climbers, such predators as weasels and foxes know that if they can strike with sufficient speed and silence they often can divide a family gang before all its members can reach safety, selecting the easiest target for their meal. But that is part of the evolutionary game plan: the healthiest and strongest generally escape, assuring the species of continued genetic safety.

* * *

The distant whine of a snowmobile punctuates the afternoon stillness and a few minutes later a Warden Service plane banks overhead, its occupants intently scanning the white landscape below for marauding dogs.

The snowmobile and the single-engine plane gone, the quiet returns to the hemlock-studded ridge that rises from the beech grove. In past winters, the ridge has served as the major thoroughfare for the back forty deer herd, but this winter it is nearly barren of tracks and droppings.

Pausing atop the ridge, I prop my pack basket against the trunk of a dead hemlock. Filled with salted apple quarters and cracked corn, the pack weighs close to 60 pounds and the hike up the steep, icy flank of the ridge had been anything but leisurely.

The almost total absence of deer signs is puzzling. Those few signs that can be detected are at least two weeks old. And there is not even a slight depression in the snow where in past winters there had always been a path so constantly used that it bottomed out on bare ground, regardless of the snow depth.

Dogs have been roaming the woods and fields a mile or so to the north, issued licenses to kill by their ignorant owners, but there have been no signs that they have ventured into the back forty. Perhaps their proximity has nonetheless frightened the deer off their generations-old winter grounds. Where, then, are they?

Sliding a few of the apples onto low hardwood stems in the event a deer should happen by, I shoulder the pack and start down the ridge, bound for the other side of the woodlot. There are tracks at the base of the ridge, but not many. There is also the track

Deer in Winter "Yard"   Maine Fish & Game Dept.

of a single snowmobile that had left the meandering logging roads of the abutting woodlot to enter the back forty, passing within six feet of a plainly visible "No Trespassing" sign in the process. Folks in the neighborhood know the back forty is not entirely off limits, but I had thought they knew that snowmobiles and hunters — with the exception of those pursuing wounded game — are taboo. A clearly marked chain may take care of that.

Bent by the heavy snows of earlier winter, saplings and low pine boughs choke the trail, but the snowmobile and a lone cross-country skier have pushed their way through. Unsheathing my pack saw, I stop to fell the saplings and those of the pine boughs that have died, scattering the former at the sides of the trail in the hope that the deer may find their succulent buds.

One hundred yards down the trail the scattered deer tracks converge. Droppings litter the snow. Most every hardwood bud within reach and many of the evergreen tips have been eaten. And just off the trail, in the lee of the spruce grove, are the "bathtub" depressions of their beds, smooth and ice-sheathed from their body heat.

Off again comes the pack. Within 30 minutes, most every hardwood shoot within 50 yards of the beds is fruited like an image from a strange dream. Apple quarters bounce in the stiffening breeze and corn fills a half-dozen of the depressions.

Turning my steps toward the farmhouse, I imagine the deer waiting patiently in the thick, surrounding brush. Perhaps it is not my imagination.

White-tailed Deer Buck   Leonard Lee Rue III

Guy Gannett Publishing Co.

HOT & COLD

The log went into the fireplace shortly before midnight, nestled in a depression of coals and ashes. Fifteen hours later, the last of its fibers burst briefly into flame and, reduced to a blackened cinder, rolled softly onto the bricks.

It seemed as though the hefty piece of oak protested its demise, fighting throughout the night and morning to repel the consuming heat, to deny its mortality.

Its journey had begun more than 30 years before, with the swift descent of an acorn from parental limb to the damp incubator of the earth. There it had lain for a time, waiting and feeling the dampness enveloping and softening its skin.

Suddenly, its skin had burst and through the ensuing fissure crept an opaque tendril topped by a light green bundle. Pressing against the dank debris, the tendril wavered slightly, assessing its surroundings. It pressed onward toward the soft light that filtered through the debris until its bundled tip protruded, basking in the full light of a spring day.

Unfolding its first wrinkled leaves, the infant tree drank of the sunlight, straightened its stem and set about the task of asserting its claim as heir to the forest canopy. Throughout the summer months it struggled to overcome the claims of other heirs. Its stem hardened in the shadow of its burgeoning cluster of leaves. Its leaves felt the first scratching footfall of beetles, its roots the first probing caress of worms.

With the chill of autumn's approach, it clenched the membranes about the bases of its leaves and the leaves dried, browned and slipped to the earth.

Winter came and with it the greatest of tests. Bitter cold penetrated the young tree's every fiber, deer and rabbits tore at its vulnerable buds and snow burdened its would-be branches. But it prevailed and with the arrival of spring it heeded again the rejuvenating dictates of the warm sunlight. Leaves emerged from the remaining buds. Those leaves nearest the ravaged buds quickly extended their tender stems, branching and leafing and branching again.

Summer passed and autumn came. The winter winds scoured the tree. Spring. Summer. Autumn. Winter....

By its 10th year, the young oak had established its claim and no longer paid much attention to the pretentious tendrils and tiny leaves emerging from the debris in the shadows of its limbs. Its

Isabel Lewando

trunk was dark and creased with healthy wrinkles. Its leaves were legion and beyond the reach of deer and rabbits.

It was safe and others found safety in its sinewy arms.

It was both perch and nursery for untold birds. Insects squeezed into its wrinkles. Tiny wasps bored holes in its leaves to deposit their eggs, around which grew dimpled, spherical shells. Squirrels scampered through its boughs, now and then constructing ponderous nests in its upper reaches, close to its trunk. The great-great-great-grandchildren of the deer which had nibbled its buds came now to rub their antlers and flanks against its rough bark.

During the winter months, chipmunks, mice, moles and salamanders slept in the labyrinth of its roots. Woodpeckers and nuthatches hitched up and down its trunk, prying insects from its creases and wrinkles.

In its 35th year, the tree towered above its nearest kin, shading even the lichen-encrusted remnants of its parent. It had seen and felt much, yet there were many more years to see and feel.

The chain saw bit into the tree's trunk and a minute later it crashed to the damp earth. The saw bit again and again and again, severing its limbs and dividing its creased trunk into dozens of pieces, each oozing sap from its whitish flesh.

Winter came. The segments of the oak lay piled beneath the snow. No sap oozed from their whitish flesh. The spring and summer sunlight found no leaves to nurture. The birds found other limbs on which to build their nests.

Autumn passed and with it the segments of the oak were removed and piled again in a dark and musty shed atop and beneath segments of maple, birch, beech and other oak trees. The pile grew smaller as the winter weeks crept by until but one segment of the oak remained.

On a chill February night, that segment, too, disappeared.

The last of its fibers burst briefly into flame and then, reduced to a blackened cinder, rolled softly onto the bricks.

* * *

Winter hikers, campers, snowmobilers and skaters are prime candidates for a variety of ailments unique to the season, the most common of which is frostbite.

Despite its frequency, frostbite is widely misunderstood in terms of both cause and treatment and stricken persons often suffer needlessly. It is, for example, a fairly common belief that frostbite

Isabel Lewando

should be treated by rubbing the affected area with snow. Would you stick a burned hand into an oven? Hardly, but it is surprising how many people are convinced that the same principle applies to frostbite.

That particular misconception apparently stems from the fact that mild cases of frostbite can be treated by gently massaging the affected area. But there is a mighty big difference between a rubdown with snow and a gentle massage: the former can cause extensive tissue destruction and is likely to retard natural healing.

Frostbite is essentially a freezing of tissue that can occur whenever the temperature is 32 degrees (farenheit) or below, including wind chill factor. Wind is particularly threatening to exposed skin because it increases the rate at which body heat is lost. As the skin is chilled, blood vessels become obstructed and the flow of blood which maintains normal body temperature slows. Actual destruction of tissue begins when the flow of blood is altogether stopped. The deeper the frostbite, the more severe its effects.

Ears, noses and fingers are the most commonly affected extremities, not only because they are apt to be exposed to the air, but because they — and the toes — have less natural, fatty insulation than other parts of the body.

A variety of factors contribute to or accelerate the advance of frostbite and many can be avoided. Common sense is the principal weapon against the affliction, epitomized by the selection and use of appropriate clothing. Boots and gloves should not be excessively tight as that can restrict proper blood flow as effectively as can actual chilling. Mittens are far better than gloves for retaining body heat and those equipped with backings of fur or felt are good investments because the backings can be used to massage exposed areas of skin, encouraging circulation and retarding frostbite.

More than once I have been grateful for the extra pair of heavy wool socks I carry on winter hikes. Feet can and do sweat in the coldest weather and damp feet are likely to become frostbitten feet. Wearing a pair of light, thin socks under heavy woolen ones is wise because they will "wick" sweat away from the skin, a principle that applies to other undergarments as well. The extra pair of socks, jammed into a pocket or pack, can be used not only to replace sodden socks, but as emergency mittens.

Despite its superficially warming effects, liquor has no place whatsoever in the winter woods. Booze, some drugs and, to a lesser degree, tobacco are not only additional tools for slowing normal blood circulation, but they produce a disorientation and dulling of the senses that can impair one's ability to detect and cope with frostbite, not to mention a number of other perils. Amputation of a finger, hand or foot is a ridiculous price to pay for a psychological "glow."

Should frostbite occur, do not treat it outdoors unless absolutely necessary: refreezing of frostbitten extremities after a brief thawing means almost certain tissue damage. As calmly as possible, return to your car or home. Running or otherwise increasing physical exertion will only increase the rate at which valuable body heat is lost and, hence, the severity of the frostbite. Cover all affected areas, placing frostbitten hands, for example, against your armpits or inside your pants.

Once you have reached home, allow the frostbitten area to thaw at room temperature for two to three minutes before immersing it in warm — about 100 degrees farenheit — water and massaging it gently. If possible, raise the frostbitten area above you to avoid a potentially damaging rush of blood through weakened vessels.

The thawing-out process can be very painful, but that is to be expected and an absence of pain is to be considered a sign of serious damage requiring immediate attention by a physician. It is wise to have a doctor examine all frostbite cases anyway.

Do not bandage frostbitten areas unless there are open wounds or sores, in which event a doctor should handle the bandaging. Do not be concered about the eruption of small blisters on frostbitten skin that has been thawed: they are a sure sign that successful thawing has occurred and they can be expected to break in a week or less. Minor cases of frostbite usually do not produce blistering.

An absence of blistering in severe cases of frostbite, coupled with continued numbness and a lack of muscle response in the affected area means something is seriously wrong. Consult your physician immediately.

Bitter as the winds may blow and deep as the snow may drift, now is the time to lace up the insulated boots and cut that trail through the woods to grandmother's house, the trail you have been talking about for years.

Residents of rural areas have taken on city airs these days, relying ever more consistently on the automobile to convey them even the shortest of distances to visit a neighbor. What has become of hours-long treks through the snow-shrouded woods, just for the fun of it or to deliver a basket of Christmas goodies to the Smiths?

I am not much for visiting people during the winter months, but

I do enjoy a trek across the ridge to the bogs and thickets beyond. I am a bushwacker at heart, going where instinct and impulse dictate, but I appreciate the value of a good trail to those who visit the back forty to hike, snowshoe or cross-country ski. I like to tell them that "I'm going to stick by the fire: you know where the trails are."

Cutting a woods trail is no simple, afternoon task in any season, but winter cutting definitely has its benefits. For one thing, the absence of leaves on the hardwood trees makes it fairly easy to determine land contours at some distance and it is those contours or shapes that have more to do with a trail's character than anything else. Winter cutting is also recommended because the trees to be pruned or trimmed are dormant and are therefore less likely to be injured: one has only to cut a limb from a spring maple to learn just how much of the tree's vital sap can be lost when it is running.

Winter cuts are additionally advantageous because the snow-cover permits limbing and pruning to greater heights than are reasonably possible at other times of the year. Common sense dictates that a trail designed for winter use should have a higher ceiling than one meant to be used only during the spring, summer and autumn. And if you or anyone who is likely to use the trail owns a saddle horse, a high-ceilinged trail is required.

Winterbound animals appreciate a winter cut, finding shelter amid the fallen limbs and saplings. Squirrels, among others, will seek out fresh cuttings and quickly bloat themselves on what frozen hardwood sap is emitted.

The tools of the trail cutting trade are simple and few. A light, tubular metal bowsaw is a "must" and unless you enjoy sharpening your own blades buy one whose blade can be replaced. Long-handled pruning shears are occasionally helpful, especially for removing the outer portions of overhanging limbs that need not be altogether removed. Pruning scissors or "clippers" are useful only if you are a perfectionist and plan to sculpt your trail.

Chain saws are fine for cutting firewood but are virtually out of the question for trail work because they and their requisite paraphernalia are far too bulky.

The actual cutting process is reasonably simple compared to the process of deciding where to do it. One does not simply cut a straight swath through the woods, removing whatever happens to get in the way. Not only does such a trail look bad, but it defies the basic laws of movement: only crows travel "as the crow flies."

A woods trail should follow the natural contours of the land,

Guy Gannett Publishing Co.

traversing slopes rather than marching directly up them, circling sinkholes and crossing brooks at their narrowest springtime points. Keep in mind the fact that a woods trail should be a fairly leisurely thing, something that does not tax the body more than it has to. Distance is less important than utility.

There are personal considerations in the arrangement of a woods trail. If you are a birdwatcher, you probably will want your trail to provide access to a variety of terrain and growth. If you are a cross-country skier, your trail should be relatively free of sharp, hillside curves.

Once you know what you want your trail to do, fill a pocket with strips of brightly colored tape or ribbon and venture forth. Follow what you expect will be the route of your trail, affixing the markers to bushes and tree limbs. Repeat the process, making whatever adjustments are dictated by terrain and whim.

Then it is time to get to work.

If there is one cardinal rule about cutting a trail, it is a simple one. Do not hack. Prune and trim. Avoid felling entire trees unless there is no alternative or they should be removed for other reasons, such as overcrowding and disease. Cut branches and limbs close to the trunk, but do not cut more than about one-quarter of any single tree's limbs or it will have little chance of surviving.

There is one drawback to winter trail cutting, but to my way of thinking it is not a serious one. Any cutting undertaken when snow covers the ground bypasses much of the low growth. One must expect to spend at least a day, depending on the length of the trail, repeating the process in the late spring, removing whatever the April thaw has brought to light.

A woodland trail should not be an intrusion. It should be as innocuous as possible, twisting and turning according to the character of the land. It should not be superimposed on the trails used by animals during their dining forays, no matter how convenient that arrangement may seem: a trail should bring you closer to those animals, not frighten them into the next woodlot.

Speaking of next-door woodlots... Never cut a trail into someone else's land without their permission. Most woodlot owners are woodlot users who hike or snowshoe their acreage regularly and chances are that your neighbor would welcome a property-connecting trail that expands his or her range. Just ask.

Once cut, a trail does not automatically become a permanent fixture. It will require constant attention and maintenance, much of which is accomplished simply by using it. And that, after all, is what a woods trail is all about.

Guy Gannett Publishing Co.

CHANGE

Chinook. "Promise of spring" it is called in the North, a dry, warm wind sliding across the mountains, cold plateaus and canyons.

New England, too, has its chinook, though it is more intangible even than the wind; a sensation in the bones, a whisper borne on wet snowflakes and birds' tongues. It is nonetheless an equally clear flute-song of impending spring.

The first faint whisper comes from the hardwood grove behind the barn. The maple buds are fatter, sharply outlined against the blue sky where the late winter sun lengthens its daily transit. Some elderberry buds have actually split, baring the blue-green undersides of infant leaves.

The stalks of the blueberry bushes are reddening and there have been pussywillows in the large pond for several weeks.

But this has been a fickle winter, one of false promises and muffled whispers. The sense of expectation is real enough, lent premature life perhaps by an abnormal weariness with an abnormal winter.

No. The signs are real.

The chickadees are consistently singing their spring songs. "*Chee*-dee." Some call it the "false phoebe song" and it does indeed remind the listener of the diminutive flycather's vocalizations.

The males among our flock of a dozen pigeons, drawn to the country by chicken barns and other sources of food, are getting anxious, strutting about the backyard with inflated chests and trying occasionally to impress the females with their stick-gathering abilities.

The squirrels, too, are getting a bit itchy, chasing one another from treetop to treetop and chattering with an exuberance they have not shown for months.

The crows are getting noisier and cavorting above the fields on rising breezes.

The woodchuck hole behind the barn shows signs of sporadic use, though I cannot tell for certain if the 'chuck itself has been abroad.

The dark earth beneath the birdfeeders is damp and smells of spring, a heavy, musty odor that, like this transitory time itself, is intangible. It is to be sensed, not smelled.

The trees, too, have a wet, pungent smell. The smell of the evergreens never completely leaves the woods, but it changes with the seasons, becoming thicker and wetter now.

    This fickle, changeling winter may well have a few punches left, but its strength is nearly sapped and the season grows weary. Spring is coming. It is there, just beyond the ridge.

Guy Gannett Publishing Co.

BIBLIOGRAPHY

This is not a bibliography in the usual sense of the term. Rather, it is a list of those books and materials in my own library that were consulted from time to time in the preparation of the newspaper columns from which this book was conceived. These materials not only were consulted for specific information, but in many cases they suggested column topics or simply provided additional insight that was later integrated into a column or columns.

In addition to the materials listed here, I have made considerable use of such periodicals as the newsletter of the Maine Audubon Society and the magazines *Smithsonian*, *Audubon*, *National Geographic*, *American Birds* and *National Wildlife*. The library files at the Portland offices of the Guy Gannett Publishing Co. have also been used extensively, for which I extend my sincere thanks to librarian Mary Sparrow and her staff.

— Bob Niss

Allaby, Michael; *Animal Artisans;* Alfred A. Knopf, N.Y., 1982.

Ardrey, Robert; *African Genesis;* Dell Publishing Co. Inc., N.Y., 1961.

Ardrey, Robert; *The Territorial Imperative;* Dell Publishing Co. Inc., N.Y., 1966.

Bellrose, Frank C.; *Ducks, Geese and Swans of North America;* Stackpole Books, Harrisburg, Pa., 1980.

Brown, Leslie; *Eagles of the World;* Universe Books, N.Y., 1977.

Bull, John and Farrand, John Jr.; *The Audubon Society Field Guide to North American Birds* (Eastern Region); Alfred A. Knopf, N.Y., 1977.

Burton, Maurice (ed.); *The New Larousse Encyclopedia of Animal Life;* Larousse & Co. Inc., N.Y., 1980

Cahalane, Victor H. (ed.); *The Imperial Collection of Audubon Animals;* Bonanza Books, N.Y., 1967.

Campbell, Bruce; *The Dictionary of Birds;* Viking Press, N.Y., 1974.

Carson, Rachel; *Silent Spring;* Houghton Mifflin Co., Boston, 1962.

Cobb, Boughton; *A Field Guide to the Ferns and Their Related Families;* Houghton Mifflin Co., Boston, 1963.

Collins, Henry Hill Jr. (ed.); *Harper & Row's Complete Field Guide to North American Wildlife* (2 vols.); Harper & Row Publishers, N.Y., 1981.

Ellis, Richard; *The Book of Whales;* Alfred A. Knopf, N.Y., 1980.

Everett, Michael; *A Natural History of Owls;* Hamlyn Publishing Group Ltd., London, 1977.

Feduccia, Alan; *The Age of Birds;* Harvard University Press, Cambridge, 1980.

Fletcher, Colin; *The Thousand-Mile Summer;* Howell-North Books, San Diego, 1964.

Forbush, Edward Howe; *Birds of Massachusetts and Other New England States* (3 vols.); Norwood Press, Norwood, 1925.

Fox, H. Munro; *The Personality of Animals;* Penguin Books, Baltimore, 1952.

Gibbons, Euell; *A Wild Way to Eat;* Hurricane Island Outward Bound School, 1967.

Gibbons, Euell; *Stalking the Wild Asparagus;* David McKay & Co. Inc., N.Y., 1971.

Gibbons, Euell; *Stalking the Blue-Eyed Scallop;* David McKay & Co. Inc., N.Y., 1964.

Godfrey, Earl W.; *The Birds of Canada;* National Museum of Natural Sciences, National Museums of Canada, Ottawa, 1979.

Graham, Frank; *Gulls (A Social History);* Random House, N.Y., 1975.

Griscom, Ludlow and Sprunt, Alexander Jr.; *The Warblers of America;* Doubleday & Co. Inc., Garden City, N.Y., 1979.

Harrison, Hal H.; *A Field Guide to Birds' Nests (In the United States East of the Mississippi River);* Houghton Mifflin Co., Boston, 1975.

Hellyer, A.G.L.; *Shrubs in Colour;* Collingridge Books, London, 1965.

Hickman, Mae and Guy, Maxine; *Care of the Wild Feathered & Furred: A Guide to Wildlife Handling & Care;* Unity Press, Santa Cruz, 1973.

Janovy, John Jr.; *Yellowlegs;* Houghton Mifflin Co., Boston, 1980.

Johnsgard, Paul A.; *Grouse and Quails of North America;* University of Nebraska Press, Lincoln, 1973.

Kimball, John W.; *Cell Biology;* Addison-Wesley Publishing Co., Reading, Mass., 1970.

Krieger, Louis C.C.; *The Mushroom Handbook;* Dover Publications Inc., N.Y., 1967.

Letourneau, Gene L.; *Sportsmen Say;* Guy Gannett Publishing Co., Augusta, Me., 1975.

MacGowan, Kenneth and Hester, Joseph A. Jr.; *Early Man in the New World;* Doubleday & Co. Inc., Garden City, N.Y., 1962.

Martin, Alfred G.; *Hand-Taming Wild Birds at the Feeder;* Bond Wheelwright Co., Freeport, Me., 1963.

Moore, Patrick; *The Rand McNally New Concise Atlas of the Universe;* Rand McNally & Co., N.Y., 1978.

Morris, Desmond; *The Naked Ape;* Dell Publishing Co. Inc., N.Y., 1967.

Nuttall, Thomas: *A Popular Handbook of the Ornithology of Eastern North America;* Little Brown & Co., John Wilson & Son, Cambridge, 1896.

Palmer, Ralph S. (ed.); *Handbook of North America Birds (Vol. 1, Loons through Flamingos);* Yale University Press, New Haven, 1976.

Parry, Gareth and Putnam, Rory; *Birds of Prey;* Simon and Schuster, N.Y., 1979.

Pearson, T. Gilbert (ed.); *Birds of America;* Garden City Books, Garden City, N.Y., 1936.

Peterson, Roger Tory; *A Field Guide to the Birds;* Houghton Mifflin Co., Boston, 1980.

Peterson, Roger Tory and McKenny, Margaret; *A Field Guide to the Flowers of Northeastern and North-Central America;* Houghton Mifflin Co., Boston, 1968.

Petrides, George A.; *A Field Guide to the Trees and Shrubs;* Houghton Mifflin Co., Boston, 1972.

Pettingill, Olin Sewall Jr.; *Ornithology in Laboratory and Field;* Burgess Publishing Co., Minneapolis, 1970.

Phillips, David and Nash, Hugh (eds.); *The Condor Question;* Friends of the Earth, 1981.

Pyle, Robert Michael; *The Audubon Society Field Guide to North American Butterflies;* Alfred A. Knopf, N.Y., 1981.

Riviere, Bill, et al; *The L.L. Bean Guide to the Outdoors;* Random House, N.Y., 1981.

Rutstrum, Calvin; *Paradise Below Zero;* The MacMillan Co., N.Y., 1968.

Rutstrum, Calvin; *The Wilderness Cabin;* The MacMillan Co., N.Y., 1961.

Sagan, Carl; *Cosmos;* Random House, N.Y., 1980.

Schuler, Stanley; *The Gardener's Basic Book of Trees & Shrubs;* Simon & Schuster, N.Y., 1973.

Smoot, Robert C. and Price, Jack and Barrett, Richard L.; *Chemistry (A Modern Course);* Charles E. Merrill Books Inc., Columbus, Ohio, 1965.

Teale, Edwin Way; *North With the Spring;* Dodd, Mead and Co., N.Y., 1951.

Terres, John K.; *The Audubon Society Encyclopedia of North American Birds;* Alfred A. Knopf, N.Y., 1980.

Todd, Frank S.; *Waterfowl — Ducks, Geese & Swans of the World;* Sea World Press and Harcourt Brace Janovich, N.Y., 1979.

Truslow, Frederick Kent; *The Nesting Season;* Viking Press, N.Y., 1979.

Tweedie, Michael; *The World of Dinosaurs;* William Morrow and Co. Inc., N.Y., 1977.

Walker, Lewis Wayne; *The Book of Owls;* Alfred A. Knopf, N.Y., 1974.

Willmore, Sylvia Bruce; *Swans of the World;* Taplinger Publishing Co., N.Y., 1974.

Field Notes

Field Notes

Field Notes

Field Notes